SAS

WHO DARES WINS

LEADERSHIP SECRETS FROM
THE SPECIAL FORCES

Anthony Middleton, Jason Fox,
Matthew Ollerton and Colin Maclachlan

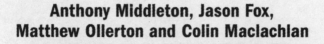

SAS

WHO DARES WINS

LEADERSHIP SECRETS FROM THE SPECIAL FORCES

MINNOW FILMS

HEADLINE

First published in 2016
by HEADLINE PUBLISHING GROUP

This paperback edition published in 2017
by HEADLINE PUBLISHING GROUP

11

Cataloguing in Publication Data is available from the British Library

ISBN 978 1 4722 4073 6

MINNOW FILMS

Additional photographs courtesy of the DS

Typeset in Akzidenz Grotesque by CC Book Production

Printed and bound in Great Britain by CPI Group (UK) Ltd, Croydon, CR0 4YY

Headline's policy is to use papers that are natural, renewable and
recyclable products and made from wood grown in well-managed forests
and other controlled sources. The logging and manufacturing processes
are expected to conform to the environmental regulations
of the country of origin.

MIX
Paper from
responsible sources
FSC® C104740

HEADLINE PUBLISHING GROUP
An Hachette UK Company
Carmelite House
50 Victoria Embankment
London EC4Y 0DZ

www.headline.co.uk
www.hachette.co.uk

To the extraordinary men and women we had the honour
to serve alongside during our military careers. This book
is dedicated to those who supported us to achieve things
we never thought possible, who returned with injuries both
visible and invisible, and to those who never came home.

And to our families and friends at home for their enduring
love and support – we couldn't have done it without you.

CONTENTS

PART THREE
CONFLICT

PART FOUR
TEAMWORK, LEADERSHIP
AND RESPONSIBILITY

PART FIVE
BECOMING THE
THINKING SOLDIER

GLOSSARY OF TERMS AND ABBREVIATIONS

CASEVAC – casualty evacuation

CO – Commanding Officer

contact – to intercept or engage with the enemy

DS – Directing Staff: the assessors for SAS Selection

extract – to remove personnel from a combat zone

Green Army – the Regular Army

high-threat detention mission – a mission where the aim is to detain a high-risk target such as a Taliban leader

IED – improvised explosive device

IED facilitator – someone who helps to build and distribute IEDs

intel – intelligence

noisy – a firefight: 'It got noisy in there pretty quickly.'

NVGs – night vision goggles

pass out – to complete a military course

point man – a soldier who leads a unit into a hostile position

Quick Reaction Force (QRF) – a unit designed to provide a rapid response in unfolding situations

rebomb – to reload a weapon

SAS – Special Air Service

SBS – Special Boat Service

tour – a tour of duty: time spent in a hostile area, such as Iraq or Afghanistan

walk-in operation – a mission where a unit arrives on foot

wet, a – a hot drink. The word for a cup of tea in the Marines; in the Army, it's known as a 'brew'

PREFACE

'WHO DARES WINS': it's long been our motto in the British Special Forces, a highly skilled unit of the military's most effective soldiers. For much of our history, that one pithy statement has made for an apt summary of how we operate in the field of combat – *we dare, we win.* In times of crisis, such as the infamous Iranian Embassy siege of 1980, in which 26 people were taken captive by terrorists, our operatives were deployed to resolve a pressurised hostage situation with force. In warzones, we're dropped behind enemy lines in order to wreak havoc, killing high-profile targets and disrupting dangerous weapons systems on command. As far as the military are concerned, we've long been regarded as being the best of the best.

There's more to a life in the Special Forces than simply exercising extreme violence, however. Our secretive work isn't only about aggression and selfless acts of bravery, though everybody in the Regiment is aware of the risks that face us in a theatre of war, where death, capture and torture are very real possibilities. Instead, we like to think of ourselves as 'Thinking Soldiers': individuals built to be both leaders and team players; schemers capable of adapting to any situation; Jacks and masters of all trades with a chameleon-like ability to blend into any situation undetected.

That is the reason why so many civilians are fascinated by the SAS and SBS. Countless books have been written about our work; feature films and documentaries have been made, too. The uniform probably helps. The Regiment's all-black get-up and balaclavas carry an air of sophisticated menace, though a lot of the interest in our work focuses on the operations we execute and the physical hardships we endure along the way. A lot of people want to know exactly how tough somebody has to be to pass Selection, the gruelling entrance trial that works as a gateway into the Special Forces.

Over two seasons, our Channel 4 TV show, *SAS: Who Dares Wins*, has set out to do exactly that. Gathering together groups of civilian 'recruits', many of whom were considered to be at the peak of physical fitness, we pushed them through a diluted version of Selection over eight days. They suffered the same physical hardships, mental fatigue and emotional breakdowns experienced by most soldiers while attempting to make it into the Special Forces. Along the way, all of them learned something about their personal abilities as leaders and team players, whether they made it through to the finishing line (which very few did) or dropped out at the first stage. Strengths were highlighted, weaknesses exposed. As a result they became better leaders, better team players, *better people*, when they were returned to 'Real Life'.

In the pages of *SAS: Who Dares Wins – Leadership Secrets from the Special Forces*, we've distilled those same lessons, and many others, into a handbook for people of responsibility at all levels. It might be that you're the CEO of a multinational company or the founder of a new start-up; maybe you want to improve your communication skills as the manager of a local football team, or you're working as the new boss in a job where the mechanics and personalities of your group seem unfamiliar and have placed you outside your comfort zone. Either way, this book will deliver a series of battle-hardened leadership techniques for you to utilise, each one learned under pressure.

Split into five core sections, the book will detail the experiences that have led us, the four members of the show – Ant Middleton, Jason Fox, Matthew Ollerton and Colin Maclachlan – towards a life in the Special Forces, plus the hardships and lessons we had to experience in Selection before joining up with the toughest military unit in the world. From there we'll share our techniques with you on the subjects of 'Mission Planning'; 'Conflict'; 'Teamwork, Leadership and Responsibility'; and 'Becoming the Thinking Soldier'. Each chapter will tackle a leadership issue head on, such as how to handle a worst-case scenario or the techniques required to remain calm under extreme pressure. We'll then deliver anecdotal evidence on how we resolved those same issues within conflicts, before breaking down the skills that are transferrable into a civilian context.

With our help you can operate with the same precision and efficiency as the Thinking Soldier.

You can become elite.

THE DS

MEET THE DS

ANTHONY 'ANT' MIDDLETON

Ant joined the Royal Engineers in 1997 at the age of 16. He left them in 2002 to serve with the Royal Marines and was deployed to Afghanistan as a section commander. Having passed UK Special Forces Selection (Selection) at the first attempt, in 2008 he joined the SBS, where he was deployed twice more to Afghanistan as a point man and team leader until 2011.

During the early stages of his Special Forces career, Ant would lead the team across terrain and into enemy-occupied buildings where there was often close-quarters combat. Elsewhere, he was utilised as a helicopter sniper and narrowly escaped death while serving in Afghanistan, when several rounds of returning enemy fire missed his head by a matter of centimetres.

Ant now works in the mining and security sector in Africa, as well as with several charity operations throughout the continent, providing clean water and drilling and constructing wells for villages and communities that have been affected by serious water shortages.

MATTHEW 'OLLIE' OLLERTON

Ollie joined the Royal Marine Commandos in 1990 at the age of 18 and served in Northern Ireland. On his first day on duty, a 500lb car bomb exploded in a nearby checkpoint, killing everybody inside. Ollie was tasked with clearing the wreckage. A year later, he served in Operation Desert Storm in Iraq, during which he evacuated Kurds from a number of villages that had been destroyed in the conflict.

In 1994, Ollie completed Selection and joined the SBS, where he worked globally on operations and participated in marine counterterrorism missions.

Ollie retired from the Special Forces and worked as a Country Manager for a private security company (PSC) in Iraq, and later as an Operations Manager helping to free children held in sex-trafficking camps across south-east Asia. Alongside Jason Fox, he currently runs Break-Point, a group which introduces corporate business leaders to the techniques and tactics used by the British Special Forces.

JASON 'FOXY' FOX

Foxy joined the Royal Marines when he was 16 and worked his way up to Selection, which he passed in 2002. He completed multiple tours of Afghanistan as well as serving globally on numerous operations in the SBS, as a demolitions expert, combat swimmer and dog handler.

Foxy left the SBS as a Sergeant in 2012 when he was diagnosed with post-traumatic-stress disorder. He later attributed his condition to the pressures of frequent tours during which his life was constantly under threat. He now prepares film and television production crews operating in high-risk zones.

With Ollie, he runs a company called Break-Point, which introduces corporate business leaders to the techniques and tactics used by the British Special Forces.

COLIN MACLACHLAN

Colin joined the military in 1989, when he was 15. His military life began with the Royal Scots; he later gained the rank of Warrant Officer Class II. He was put up for Selection to the SAS in 1998 and became the first person to pass into the Special Forces from his regiment in 20 years. Colin operated in the Balkans, Afghanistan and the UK.

After leaving the SAS, Colin moved back to Edinburgh. He now works as a Risk Management Consultant. He is also a TV presenter, author and ambassador for several charities, including Pilgrim Bandits, the Lee Rigby Foundation, the NSPCC and the Leeds Rhinos Foundation.

PART ONE
JOINING THE ELITE

1

WHO DARES WINS: JOINING THE SAS

No matter what we do in life, most of us strive to fulfil our potential; there's an innate desire to operate at the peak of our abilities, whether that be at work, at home, working on our physical fitness or even handling our finances. Politicians want to lead at the highest levels, footballers dream of playing in the World Cup, entrepreneurs have an urge to score the biggest deals. Meanwhile, all of us like to be recognised for hard work or given credit for our efforts and ideas.

Personal achievement – big and small – is what drives us and it's no different in the military. For a number of soldiers, merely functioning in the theatre of combat isn't enough. We want to be the best of the best, and the only way to get there is to join the Special Forces.

COLIN: It takes a lot to become a member of the Special Forces – the British military's elite regiment. When the corps first started, during the Second World War, it was as a commando force that worked behind enemy lines during the campaign in North Africa. Later, its primary tasks became hostage rescue, counterterrorism, intelligence gathering, sabotage and direct-action operations. Because of the undercover nature of its work, personnel had to be of elite quality. There was no room for weakness, so each soldier joining 'The Regiment' – as it was nicknamed – came quickly to be regarded as the best of the best.

Meanwhile, everyone involved possessed a combination of unique qualities, allowing him to perform high-risk tasks under extreme pressure. These included basic requirements, such as expert soldiering skills and leadership qualities. But there were valuable personal characteristics that individuals had to possess if they were to pass Selection – the gruelling series of tests that established whether a soldier had the minerals to join the Special Forces. These included adaptability to change, humour and humility, attention to detail, mental strength and a positive attitude, passion and lateral thinking. It wasn't just about being the bravest or the fittest. (Though those characteristics were undoubtedly helpful.) It was about being the 'Thinking Soldier', and using brains over brute force.

I had always wanted to operate at the top end in the military. It was one thing to guard Balmoral Castle as a soldier; it was an altogether different experience to rescue hostages held at a military stronghold in Iraq. Like anyone who takes pride in their profession, I wanted to perform at the highest level and be recognised as part of the elite. That's the same for a lot of people: an ambitious stockbroker would want to work at one of the biggest companies in London or New York, for example. In the British Army there was only one place to go if you wanted to be regarded as one of the very best, and that was the Special Forces. It wasn't just the pride of the Army, but of the Navy and RAF, too.

I had joined the military at the age of 15; my mum had told me that she wanted me out of the house at 16, so I signed up for the Army with two weeks to go. I was petrified at first. The job could be quite scary and lonely at times; I was getting wet and dirty, and putting cam [camouflage] cream on for £5 a week. I ended up with the Royal Scots and completed my training in preparation for the first Iraq war.

I later learned that nobody had passed Selection from our unit in a generation. (Nobody else has passed since my entering the Special Forces.) There was a mystique about the SAS, and, like a lot of my mates, I had read the famous SAS books, such as Andy McNab's *Bravo Two Zero*, which only fuelled my fascination, and the thought of a different way of life in the military excited me. Working at the top end was much more appealing than marching around a field in South Armargh or patrolling the streets of Belfast, which were regular drills during our conflict with the IRA.

To volunteer for Selection, I had to apply through the Royal Scots. Some units have their own 'beat-up' to get there – a mini-Selection that establishes if a soldier is truly up to the tasks ahead. There hadn't been any of that in the Royal Scots, though; guys weren't banging on the Commanding Officer's door to join the SAS, so nobody thought to have an entry course, and when I announced my decision in 1998 it was considered a rarity. I was given a couple of weeks prior to Selection so I could work on navigation practice and fitness drills, which was useful, but my first day on Selection shattered any illusions that I might be one of the more advanced in the group.

When I arrived in the cookhouse at Brecon Beacons – a military camp based in the South Wales mountain range (which is quite near to the Regiment's headquarters in Hereford) and one of the locations for the recruitment process's notorious Hill Phase – nearly 200 blokes had gathered together. They arrived in all shapes and sizes. Some of them were *huge*; all of them were athletic. One or two of the guys even wore triathlon and marathon T-shirts. I was well known in my unit for being fairly fit, but on that first day I felt average. Joining the SAS was going to be a lot harder than I'd ever imagined.

FOXY: I loved soldiering. I was quietly confident and determined; I liked taking calculated risks, so I figured I could work quite well in the Special Forces. I came from a military family and joined the Marines at the age of 16. My granddad was in the Navy; my dad was in the Marines, my brother, too, so their influence and stories encouraged me to sign up.

Ten years into my career, I put myself forward for Selection, having read about the Special Forces in magazines and books.

'Fuck, that's cool,' I thought. 'I want to do that.'

I had been attracted to the Special Forces by their roguish element. Joining up would allow me to do a lot of the cool shit boys often dreamed about, and once I'd passed, I worked as a counterterrorism and demolitions expert with the Special Boat Service. At times the work was fun.

I loved the fact that the guys involved with the Special Forces had more responsibility. There was an increased sense of autonomy, too, which I liked, and an individual's ideas and opinions were valued in the Special Forces; rank meant very little. But when it came to Selection, I cuffed it. I was set to start in January. That meant I had a whole period of Christmas leave to prepare, but rather than training hard, I went on the piss and ate loads of crap food instead.

'I might as well,' I thought, trying to convince myself that I could get away with slacking. 'I've seen people over-train before Selection and they get injured quickly.'

Once I'd started, it was obvious I wasn't in the best of shape. Still, I focused on staying with the other recruits for the first two weeks. My plan was to come into my own in the second fortnight and hopefully pass that way.

OLLIE: I was part of a military family from Burton-upon-Trent in Staffordshire. My grandfather was a captain in the Royal Engineers, and my brother became a helicopter pilot with the Royal Navy, so I was always heading that way, too, especially as I was a bit of a rebel at school. I would scrap with other kids and bunk lessons; I needed discipline.

My childhood was stressful, though. Mum and Dad divorced when I was young and my grandparents passed away shortly afterwards. Then, when I was ten years old, I was mauled by a circus chimpanzee. The experience was terrifying. There was a loud scream from the monkey, all 60 kilos of it, as it pinned me to the floor, blood dripping from its teeth as it gored my flesh. That experience changed me to some degree, and as a result I suffered from post-traumatic-stress disorder.

The military saved me from really going off the rails in a way. I always wanted to serve my country, and I always wanted to be the best of the best. I eventually joined the Royal Marines at the age of 18, though when I first applied, I felt very disillusioned. Forces life didn't seem like my thing. When I talked through my military future in the Careers Office, I was asked, 'What do you want to do once you get into the Marines?' There was a book on the desk in front of me. On the open page was a photograph of a combat swimmer in the Special Boat Service.

'I want to do that,' I said, pointing at the photograph.

The Careers Officer just laughed. 'Yeah,' he said. 'They all say that.'

That always stuck with me. (Little did that Careers Officer realise that one day I would be that combat swimmer.)

Once I'd made it into the Marines, my sense of disillusionment only intensified: I hated the hierarchy and the regimental crap that came with it. I think a lot of people who go into the Special Forces feel that way. I felt frustrated, so frustrated that for a while I considered quitting the military full stop. But there was a desire to push myself harder. Everybody has a warrior spirit somewhere inside them. (Though some people have to dig really deep to find it.) For me, I wanted to be at the elite level of the job. I knew by joining the Special Forces I'd find an increased sense of satisfaction, valour – *everything*.

I also wanted to take risks and work on operations that were much more dangerous than anything I'd done with the Marines. That was my incentive. Whenever I explained to people how much I loved being in the Special Forces, they always said, 'Yeah, but you have to go to war.' But that's exactly what I wanted. With greater risks come greater rewards. That's the same in any situation: if you're not prepared to take risks in life, you won't feel fulfilled.

When I first announced that I wanted to get into the Selection process, people doubted me. The Sergeant I was working for at the time even laughed.

'Oh, this is going to be hilarious,' he said.

That gave me the fuel to push on. Desire was the quality I needed if I was to pass through: I had to be determined and able to negate any thoughts that were holding me back, and so I used other people's doubts as power. It was the incentive to get me over the line.

ANT: I grew to hate the Army, mainly towards the back end of my time there.

Prior to joining I was living in France with my family, and signing up had been an excuse to get back to England. Once my training began, I loved it and I was really looking forward to seeing how my career would unfold. Within six months of arriving at my unit (9 Parachute Squadron Royal Engineers), I knew it wasn't for me. For starters, there were lots of pub soldiers around at the time, blokes who would booze all night and then end up drinking a pint of piss for a laugh. A regular 'game' was for one of the lads to dangle their bollocks over a pool table pocket. Somebody would then fire a cue ball at them, usually as hard as possible.

I wasn't into that.

I had plenty of confidence at that time, probably too much, and it held me back initially. I'd started as a Para-trained soldier, having passed P Company, which was based in Catterick, North Yorkshire, at the Infantry Training Centre, and my ego was problematic. My confidence was confused with arrogance, which put a lot of people off me.

That came from my upbringing. As a kid I was a very outgoing person; I was popular at school, probably because I'd been brought up with older brothers to protect me, so when it came to meeting new people or working with others, I was full of self-confidence. I was self-assured and happy to let everybody know it. Don't get me wrong, I wasn't a runaway toe rag, but I definitely had some attitude.

I carried that into the Army, though what I hadn't realised

was that I needed to be a team player to progress quickly. Instead I failed to harness my confidence in the right way. I wanted to be the centre of attention, and that held me back. If I could have focused more on the job in hand rather than thinking I was better than everyone and not caring what my peers thought, I would have got a lot further, a lot faster.

There were other occasions when I felt like I was being pushed about, just for trying to get ahead. When I first joined, the unit was out on a run one day. I was right up at the front when suddenly I felt a whack around the back of my legs. I fell off the road and into a ditch. When I looked up, one of the old boys was glaring down at me.

'Fucking hell, you spod,' he hissed. 'What are you doing at the front? Get to the back. You're showing the rest of us up.'

I couldn't get my head around that. I thought, 'How are you supposed to get the best out of people if you're going to tell the enthusiastic ones not to bother?' That pissed me off, big time. I had a bolder vision for my military life than simply fitting in with everybody else. I knew I had to reach a higher level if I was to be happy, so at the age of 24 I joined the Marines.

The camaraderie and professionalism there were a lot more in tune with where I wanted to be, and I suppose that's when I first considered the idea of joining the Special Forces. But the Marines' training programme was already considered to be one of the hardest in the world. It was a massive stepping-stone. I learned exactly how far I could push myself, and how important self-belief was in driving a person forward, but only when it was under control.

Life changed once I'd passed out in 2002. After that, I didn't need to mouth off. I could prove myself on the battlefield instead; I was able to display my worth on missions. The bragging stopped. I'd reached a stage in my life where I was a father, working in Afghanistan as a Section Commander and somebody who was considered to be a good operator on the ground. Finally I felt comfortable with what I was doing.

That's when I pushed for Selection.

2

THE HILLS

Success doesn't come easily, not usually anyway. Not in life, and definitely not in the military. To reach the very apex of our abilities we sometimes have to first understand the extent of our strengths and weaknesses. The best way to do that is to springboard up from rock bottom – a place where we doubt ourselves and our resources. Clawing our way out of that uncomfortable place can be painful, though, especially when quitting often seems like the easiest escape route. But only through pushing through can we truly know what we're capable of.

The Selection process is designed to force a soldier to those low points. The difference between the ones who qualify and those who don't is usually the ability to recognise their mental weaknesses and physical flaws and then push through to the end regardless. In a work setting, that could be the seemingly insurmountable tower of paperwork before a career-defining presentation. In a personal challenge, such as a marathon, it's the final, gruelling training run that might knock our confidence when assessing our chances of getting across the finishing line.

During Selection, soldiers are challenged on a daily basis, often from the minute we begin the Hills Phase – the assessment's brutal opening section. This examination teaches us everything we need to know about the pressures that come with being in the Special Forces. Meanwhile, it's our chance to show those in charge that we've got it in us to be the very best.

ANT: Selection was the hardest thing I've ever done in my life and at times it pushed me to my limits, both mentally and physically. It was not nice. Taking place over the course of a year, it comprised five key stages:

1. The Briefing Course
2. Aptitude Phase (The Hills Phase)
3. Jungle; Special Forces Tactics, Techniques and Procedures (TTP) and Special Operations (SOP) Training
4. Survive, Evade, Resist, Extract
5. Continuation Training

At any stage, soldiers who find the workload too gruelling can bin themselves off the assessment. Likewise, should any recruits not match the expectations of the Directing Staff (the assessors) on any of the exercises, they can be thrown off Selection, especially if it looks like they might put themselves, or others, at risk.

All Selections start the same, though, with a one-week Briefing Course in which a group of hopefuls are told exactly what's expected of them should they be among the few who make it into the Special Forces. There are combat fitness tests and load marches, plus examinations of swimming, first aid, and map and compass skills. Any recruits not matching the basic criteria are usually found out pretty quickly; they're kicked off before the serious work begins. All the soldiers are given a training plan to get themselves in shape for the Selection process proper, but nothing really prepares you for the opening physical stage: 'The Hills'.

This 'aptitude phase', which is designed to push your body to its physical limits, takes place in the Brecon Beacons, a challenging range of peaks in Wales. There are two tests a year (though a soldier will only take one), one in the winter, one in the summer. The theory goes that if you get a winter Hills (when it always pisses down with rain and it's freezing cold), you'll do the Jungle Phase in the summer, which is perceived to be a better option because it takes place during the dry season. That's bullshit. I did the winter Hills and it pissed down. I did the Jungle Phase in the dry season and it also pissed down – *every day*. It was horrendous. At no stage did I ever seriously consider quitting, but there were definitely one or two occasions when I wondered out aloud, 'Why am I doing this?'

The Hills Phase was seriously hard work. There were more Basic Combat Fitness Tests, plus a series of runs and timed marches over the Brecon Beacons. Some of them, such as the final march, called 'The Endurance', required us to cover large distances in a limited amount of time. All of this was done while carrying heavy bergens and a rifle. Then there were swimming and underwater assessments. It wasn't nice at all.

Every day our basic infantry skills were tested under pressure, and questions were asked of us all the time. Can you cover excessive distances, on your own, while being self-sufficient? Can you navigate alone and get to the checkpoints you've been assigned? Can you do all that under the weight of equipment, food and water? We were allowed to haul as many provisions as we liked on the marches and runs. However, the more we carried, the more it weighed. My trick was to drink a lot through the night, maybe something every couple of hours. I was so well hydrated by morning that I wouldn't have to carry that much water during the walks and runs. We were on the hills for five or six hours, day after day, and there were several crushing moments.

COLIN: I hung on in there during the Hills Phase. Weirdly, I struggled the most in the first week. I was usually very good with a pack on my back, especially when running up steep and challenging terrain, but we did our Hills Phase in the winter and the conditions were really tough. I often found myself running, or marching, in the centre of a pack of 200 soldiers in the early stages. That position never seemed to change. With every run, I was somewhere in the middle.

Luckily, the pack reduced in size every week, and at the end everyone else around me had fallen away and I had passed. In fact, none of the guys who made it through the Hills Phase during my Selection were what you would call pack leaders at any stage. All of them were like me: on the face of it they didn't seem particularly special. They weren't really fast, muscular or incredibly clever. They were Mr Averages; strong *all-rounders*.

The weather was awful on the Brecon Beacons. Given the choice I would have much preferred the summer Hills. Sure, it's hot and really dry; a soldier has to carry a lot of fluids around, and it can be hard to make the checkpoints in time because of the fatigue, but it's still a damn sight better than winter. We were running in snow, gale force winds and horizontal rain. While working through the marches and runs people became lost on the hills. Some nearly died from hypothermia. One or two guys were found wandering on roads that were 30 or so miles wide of their checkpoints. That's how much the conditions had affected them. It was carnage.

Meanwhile, the Directing Staff played a series of mind games on us, just to add to the pressure. On one overnight march, we hiked through an awful rainstorm. The entire group were cold, wet and starving hungry by the time we arrived at our checkpoint. That's when one of the DS broke the awful news: our meal truck hadn't arrived.

'We won't be stopping for dinner,' he said. 'Get your-selves ready to go on a night NAVEX [navigation expedition]. In half an hour, I'll give the first grid references to you.'

Talk about soul-destroying!

Within half an hour of us learning the news, eight people had thrown in the towel. The realisation that there would be no food had broken them. Not long after the last one dropped out, I was told to get my checkpoint grids and jump into a truck along with several other soldiers. As soon as the seats were full, we were driven back to base. It turned out there had been no real plans for a NAVEX. The whole thing was a trick to separate the mentally tough from the weak.

We later re-created that idea during the first season of *SAS: Who Dares Wins*. Amongst the civilians hoping to make it through to the end of the show was a 'mole' – a former Marine pretending to be one of the guys. He was strong, fit, smart and likeable. On our order he threw in the towel, even though it had seemed to everybody else that he was working through the tasks quite comfortably. The psychological effect was powerful. Three or four of the recruits thought, 'Well, if he can't carry on, how the hell can I?' They dropped out immediately.

I remained strong. The Hills Phase had taught me that I didn't need to be faster, tougher or smarter than anyone else. I just had to rely on my own mental and physical strengths to get through, rather than measuring myself against the successes and failures of those around me. It was a lesson that has served me well throughout my life, both inside the military and out.

FOXY: To keep myself going through the Hills, I remembered something a mate had told me right at the very beginning of Selection. 'If you can dig in for this short period of time,' he said, 'then you get yourself into a cool club.'

I knew he was right, so I buckled down, but it was tough work. There were several really long marches where we spent a lot of time alone. We were left to our own devices. Nobody was hounding us or shouting, and it was up to every individual on Selection to prove he was up to it.

I've learned there are two types of fun in life. Type One is where we're pissing it up, laughing with mates and chatting to girls. The stimulus is immediate, but we rarely remember it weeks or months down the line. Type Two is different. It's the stuff that seems shit at first, but when it's over, there's a sense of achievement and satisfaction. For example, very few people actually enjoy running a marathon, not while they're doing it anyway. It's hell. But afterwards the tendency is to think, 'Well, that wasn't too bad.' The pain and adversity seem hilarious; the memories become fun and those events build our character.

The Hills Phase was definitely Type Two fun.

I thought I'd blown it at one stage, though. It was Test Week and I was due to hit a checkpoint during a run, but my timings seemed screwed. I was convinced I was going to arrive late. If that were true, I'd have been kicked off the course. The weather was wet and cold, and I could see the finishing point through the rain, but it was three or four miles away, down in the valley. The ground underneath me was marshland and my boots were sinking into the swampy turf. I was lumping it over the Brecon Beacons in a right stress.

'Right, I'm going to have to make a charge for it here,' I thought as I pushed forward.

My arms pumped; my legs were in agony. It was horrendous. At one point I felt like crying, but I got to the checkpoint with time to spare. In the end, it turned out I hadn't screwed up at all. I had been on time, but because the physical efforts required to get through Selection were so demanding, my mind had freaked out. Still, there was no point in getting angry. It was over.

What a bloody relief.

OLLIE: I did the Hills Phase twice because I blew my first shot at Selection [an applicant is allowed two] during the Survive, Evade, Resist, Extract Phase – the very last leg. That was crushing. I was right at the very end, avoiding capture in the Scottish wilds, where one of the rules was that we weren't allowed contact with civilians, or civilian buildings, as we tried to avoid capture.

Our patrol had been hiding out in a barn when we bumped into a farmer and his handyman. It wasn't uncommon for them to encounter soldiers on their land during Selection, and they seemed very happy to drive us to the next checkpoint. We were dropped off at the hill, out of view from the watching DS, but as we ran into the darkness, I heard a bang. I didn't think anything of it. I thought maybe the car door had been shut heavy-handedly.

A couple of days later, we were all pulled in for interrogation and read the riot act. Apparently, our farmer had been pissed, and as we bundled away from the car he had fallen over (that banging noise), smashing his head on the pavement. To get out of trouble (maybe for drink driving), he then made up a story for the local police that he'd been beaten up by the SAS. He even described us. Those notes were then passed on to the DS, and as a result our patrol was blamed and returned to unit. We had failed two days before passing the course. I later learned that everybody did what we'd been hammered for doing; they all cheated. The trick was not to get caught.

A lot of people would have been disheartened by a fall at the final hurdle. I certainly felt pretty low. But then the doubting words of my Sergeant ('Oh, this is going to be hilarious') returned. They had been a driving force throughout my lowest points on Selection; I had been desperate to prove him wrong. Those same emotions hit me when I later debated whether to take my second attempt or not. I became fired up again.

Fuck him – I'm going for it.

I wanted to get back on the horse while the blood was still fast-flowing. I knew the longer I left it, the harder it would be to pass through; I also understood I had been incredibly unlucky not to make it during my first attempt. Doing it a second time would feel a lot easier because I had experience – well, in theory anyway. I remember 250 people started on my second Hills Phase, and only seven completed Selection, but one of them was me, and, bloody hell, it was tough.

We would run night expeditions. Having returned to base

for a few hours' kip, it wasn't uncommon for us to be woken for a 'beasting', which were some of the hardest psychological thrashings I can remember. It was savage. The DS would ask us all sorts of questions and I remember being hammered one night for being unable to recall the registration details of a car that had passed us several hours previously. After that, I made a point of memorising the number plate of every car that passed me. I still do. It's a force of habit. Some events on Selection never leave you, no matter how hard you try to forget.

3

IN THE THICK OF IT

'Just how good do you want to be?'

It's a question that's asked of all of us at one stage of our life or another. Do you have the minerals to cut it as a parent, a team player, a salesman, a negotiator or a leader? And can your skill sets function effectively when they're most needed?

To be the best of the best in the British Army, it's vital as a soldier that you prove you can function at the highest level in the toughest circumstances. Our skill sets are put to the test in the harshest environments, and it doesn't get much harder than the Jungle Phase, where heat, moisture and pressure can break even the best soldiers in the business.

OLLIE: I thought the Hills Phase was tough, but the Jungle Phase took Selection to a whole other level. During my time there, the candidates were split into several teams and dropped into a rainforest location. Once we were there, our tasks were to perform navigation expeditions, jungle survival skills, contact drills (in which we would be involved in live-firing weapon training) and medical techniques. These were vital. Working in the wild meant we were exposed to serious skin infections; bites and cuts had to be looked after constantly to avoid sickness.

The jungle is the ideal environment for testing any soldier. It's raw, the conditions are brutal and it's soldiering in its purest form: it separates those who are able to function effectively under incredibly difficult conditions from those who can't. If you're unable to take care of your weapon, your kit or yourself, you'll fail. And the small failures, such as disregarding the condition of your weapon or not replacing the button on your map pocket, can cause you to rot, sometimes literally. (The dampness between your toes can cause horrific sores.) If that happens, the DS will mark you down as a bag of shit.

The conditions are tough – *really* tough. It's hot and it's wet because it's so humid, and that's before the rain starts hammering down. Whenever the heavens open it's hellish. The jungle can also become very claustrophobic because we spend around four weeks operating under a canopy of trees, amongst the dense foliage. That's why it's such an intense examination of soldiering: only the best can function in those circumstances, especially when completing mock combat raids and Immediate Action (IA) drills. (We'll talk more about those in Chapter 12.)

Meanwhile, everyone is being watched 24/7, even though it might not be immediately obvious. The DS send trackers out to trail the squadrons as they work their way through the undergrowth. These guys, who are able to smell fragrances such as body odour and toothpaste from 100 metres away, study everything we do. Any instances of poor soldiering are reported back. Finding out you've been observed without you noticing can be quite stressful, but at least it puts an end to the tricks of 'DS watchers' – people who shine whenever the assessors are around, and then turn into somebody else whenever they're not. I saw a lot of those guys during the Hills Phase. They tend to get caught out very quickly in the jungle.

The rainforest environment was a great leveller for all of us, though. The whole point of Selection is discovering a soldier's true self; it's the key factor the DS are looking for in every candidate. Once that's located, they can evaluate whether a person can truly hack it in the Special Forces. If the Hills Phase chips away at people's facades, the brave face they put on for the world, then the jungle tears it down. Everyone is placed under a magnifying glass, and in extreme conditions it's impossible for anyone to use the mask they wear for civvy street.

ANT: The jungle is about infantry soldiering, and a recruit has to be on the ball 24/7. I'm talking: cam cream on (all the time), both hands on the weapon (all the time), focus, focus,

focus (all the time). If a soldier has been sweating, which they will in the heat, it's vital they should cam up as soon as they get an opportunity because even in Selection, every second is treated like a combat situation. Every piece of kit has to be squared away; it's important not to leave any shit behind when moving out on patrol or changing camp, and whenever live firing takes place, a soldier must show competency when handling a weapon and firing rounds, which we do within inches of one another without hesitancy or error.

That level of detail can grind a person down in the jungle, no matter how tough or experienced they might be, so it's important not to let up. The minute you do, a DS will inevitably appear from behind a tree to take your name. I know, because it once happened to me when I was sleeping. I was in my hammock, which is where soldiers wear their dry kit and dry trainers.* The reason for that is if we were to get bumped in the night by enemy forces, we would be ready to grab our bags and head towards the emergency exit point and then on to the predetermined rendezvous area without too much hassle.

I had been in the jungle for a few weeks and my feet were rotten. The heels were in shreds and walking was agony. That

---

*   We have two forms of kit – wet and dry. The wet is the clothing we wear during the day and it's so-called because the fabrics are soaked through with sweat, rain and moisture from the jungle. Nothing can dry it out under the canopy of a rainforest, so putting it back on in the morning when you're tired, hungry and mentally challenged can be emotional. The dry kit is what we wear to sleep at night.

night, I slipped my heel out of my trainers so I could get some air to the soggy, peeling flesh, when out of nowhere somebody squeezed my ankles. I woke up with a start. A member of the DS was staring at me.

'Middleton, why aren't your trainers on properly?'

I sat up. 'It's my heels, Staff. They're hanging out.'

He wasn't impressed. 'I'll speak to you in the morning,' he said, darkly.

'That's it,' I thought. 'I've blown it.'

For the rest of the night I tossed and turned in my hammock, convinced I was getting binned off the following day. A voice in my head kept whispering, '*I'll speak to you in the morning . . . I'll speak to you in the morning . . .*' But when I awoke, there was no tap on the shoulder and nobody popped out from the bushes for a quiet chat. For three days I was in a state of paranoia. 'When are they going to get me?' I thought over and over. But the DS never did. My dressing down didn't come around.

That was the whole point. It was the DS's plan to sow a seed of doubt. They wanted to flip me into a period of insecurity. It would have been so easy for me to think, 'Oh, I've failed . . . Why should I continue with this fucking misery? I'm going to withdraw myself, because I've blatantly blown it.' A lot of people *do* go through that process, but not me. I knew I'd fucked up, but I learned from my mistake. For the rest of the Jungle Phase I carried on as normal.

And I slept with my trainers on properly every night.

COLIN: Going into the jungle felt like a bonus for me. I had belief in my ability and a willingness to learn. Even though I had never operated in that type of environment before, I treated it as a massive learning opportunity, one that I might never get again. That was probably a massive help: I wasn't daunted by the experience. I was hungry for it.

I got off to a tough start, though. Prior to going under the canopy, we were instructed to do beach runs on the coastline nearby, which were pretty tough because not only did they involve sprints, but the work required us to perform heaves with our partners. I tried to help one bloke by lifting his legs, which was cheating, and I was spotted. The DS ordered me to do all my exercises and the exercises of my partner, by myself. I was exhausted afterwards.

Once we were in the jungle, just about every aspect of my soldiering was put under scrutiny – both mentally and physically. I remember at one point the DS approached each soldier, asking them individually who they thought was the weakest member of the group. They were gathering intel on everybody, as well as testing the mental strength of the soldiers under scrutiny. They wanted to see how somebody reacted once their peers had pointed them out as being the least effective operative. It was a clever method of planting a seed of doubt. For the weaker soldiers, it was usually enough to bring them down.

Later, we were placed under more subtle psychological examinations. Our unit was ordered to complete a CASEVAC, which was when one member of the team goes down 'injured'.

It's then the job of everybody else to get that person to a designated extraction point. Within the drill, each member of the team takes turns carrying the casualty and leading the group, so they can be individually assessed. There were several reasons for this. The first was to expose any weak leaders. From there the DS would be able to watch as the recruit either stepped up to the challenge or wilted under the pressure. Meanwhile, the soldiers working with a poor leader were also being analysed: were they team players? And were they able to assist and offer advice (the correct approach), or would they be overpowering and try to take charge?

These drills were important in seeing how a soldier might operate once the strongest member of the group had been removed. In real-life situations, a team leader can be killed or pinned down by heavy fire. In the Special Forces, it's important that everyone can step up, if required. Everybody should be a natural leader. That's one of the strengths of the Regiment.

The CASEVAC was another of my low points during Selection. We spent the whole day running with a casualty on our backs or carrying the injured soldier on a stretcher. The terrain was unforgiving and we had to race up and down hills, across cliffs and through trees. I could see other soldiers passing out and vomiting due to the physical stress; some people ended up on drips because they were so dehydrated. I think I witnessed more withdrawals at that stage than at any other point during Selection.

It was understandable really. The process was exhausting. When I couldn't walk, I crawled, unable to see because of the sweat in my eyes, drained from the heat and dehydration. But I had one thing on my mind throughout: *Colin, just put one foot in front of the other and you'll succeed.* It was enough to get me through.

FOXY: When you eventually leave the jungle, they take you out on a helicopter, and I remember flying over the tree tops and thinking, 'Thank fuck that's over. I can go home and have a normal life again. I'm not going to be assessed constantly. I'm not going to be judged on every single thing I do.'

Because that's what it's like: the jungle is a hostile, over-powering environment. But everywhere you go, the DS are in there, too, out of sight: listening, watching and taking notes. It feels like you're being tested to the utmost – a degree to which you've never been tested before – and it's intrusive.

Every day, the DS would have a meeting in which they would assess each soldier under examination. They would share notes on what they had seen and heard. They would scrutinise our weapon handling, whether our kit was clean and if we knew how to work on certain tasks. Ultimately the question they were asking themselves was: would you want that bloke to be working with you in three months' time?

They would pick on us, too. It might not be for anything serious, but if you had made a mistake, somebody would pop up and have a go at you, even for the tiniest error. A lot of the time, you hadn't even done anything wrong. The DS were simply testing you out. They wanted to see what would happen once you had been mentally hammered. It's important to watch all of the recruits operating out of their comfort zones, because in a war everybody has to work that way. We've followed that idea during the two seasons of *SAS: Who Dares Wins*. One of us would spot a recruit who was performing really well, then we would test them. We wanted to make sure they had the presence of mind, and the mental and physical ability, to persevere.

When you pass the Jungle Phase, that's when you know you can cut it as a Special Forces soldier, because you have to seriously screw up from that point to get blown out. That was drummed into me while I was in there. Before our final ten-day exercise, one of the DS, the bloke that took me through Selection, gave us a talk.

'All I want from you guys is 110 per cent for these next ten days,' he said. 'You've got this far. Then you're in the best club in the world.'

I knew it to be true. If I got through the ordeal of Selection, I would get to do some seriously cool stuff; I'd work with the best people I'd ever worked with. His last words of advice stuck with me for those ten days: 'And if you want to achieve something, just dig deep.'

That final exercise was so boring, though. When I first went on to Selection I thought I'd be like the 'Milk Tray Man', swinging through windows in a black polo neck to save damsels in distress, a box of chocolates and a machine gun strapped to my back. Instead it was a grind. But the jungle was supposed to be gruelling and monotonous. The DS didn't need a headline-grabbing hero. They wanted to see if I had the foundations to make it as a Special Forces soldier.

4

THE QUICKENING

*All of us have a talent or skill. We're in our chosen roles
because our abilities have taken us there, and no matter
what job we're involved in, those attributes are vital in
helping us to succeed. The difference between a solider
and a member of the Special Forces – or, in other words,
an expert and the elite – is the ability to work at the
highest levels under the most difficult mental pressures.
But operating to the best of our ability is a challenge,
whatever we're doing, especially when deadlines are rapidly
approaching, people around us are panicking and the threat
of failure looms large.*

Life is a different ball game altogether.
We can all learn to function effectively within

high-pressure situations, but the only way to do so is to experience them at first hand. Lawyers in the heat of a courtroom battle; city traders closing in on a deal; journalists racing for a story: the best of them learn by operating under extreme stress. In our line of work, a member of the SAS will most experience that mental tension during the final chapter of the Selection process, where all the individuals who remain are pushed to their absolute psychological boundaries and the stresses upon them are cranked up to 11 . . .

ANT: It's called the Survive, Evade, Resist and Extract Phase, and it's the most secretive part of the entire Selection process. (Though the title should give you a general idea of what a Special Forces hopeful has to endure.) We were split into groups and let loose in the Scottish Highlands, and it was our brief to evade capture by a Hunter Force – members of the DS who were well trained when it came to locating and capturing enemy soldiers. The Hunter Force were also able to call upon road vehicles, night vision goggles and sniffer dogs – so they really had the upper hand. Once we were rounded up, every soldier had to endure the Resistance to Interrogation stage, and for what seemed like an endless time. God, it was tough. I didn't know my own name by the time I'd got out of there. That's how intense it was.

The Survival Phase was excruciating. I had just come out of the jungle and my feet were still rotten. I was in agony. But I felt a sense of pride once I'd passed; it was great knowing I'd made it into the elite, though once I'd got there, the Special Forces became just like any other job. They had their routines and challenges; I wanted to excel and meet the expectation of my peers because I knew that everyone around me had also performed to the best of their abilities to get there.

That knowledge later gave me a confidence whenever I was in the middle of a shit storm. When the bullets were flying, I could look around and think, 'Yeah, we might all die here together, but at least I've died with the best soldiers in the world.'

OLLIE: I loved the Special Forces' Selection process, the same as I loved training for the Marines. In a world where you receive very little or no congratulations for your performances you have to find your own method of appraising whether you're actually meeting the standard or not. My performance marker came from watching other people fall by the wayside as I pushed towards the end. Foxy and myself used to jokingly refer to that sensation as 'the Quickening', after a scene from the 1980s science fiction film *Highlander*, in which a bunch of immortal characters battled each other; to win a fight, one warrior would have to decapitate the other. The victor would then receive a transfer of power called 'the Quickening'.

During the Hills Phase I felt a similar surge of energy every time I watched somebody failing on Selection. It sounds brutal but their time was over and I took my satisfaction from watching the super-soldiers fail, guys I used to work with. I knew they were much stronger than me or smarter than me; they were the blokes with the shiniest boots on parade. When I saw one of them stopping by the side of the path during the Hills Phase, I'd slow a little.

'Mate, are you giving up?' I'd ask.

If ever they nodded in pain, I'd feel a rush of power. Sure, I'd give them some encouragement to carry on, but I knew they were out of the game.

The Quickening.

Once I'd passed Selection I felt on top of the world, but after I'd met with my unit for the first time, it became very apparent that I actually knew fuck all. There were more lessons to go through such as combat swimming, foreign weapons training and so on. I was fresh out of the box. I only had the basics.

COLIN: We went on the run out in a Scottish forest, but it was fun! I was put into a team and our brief was to cover long distances every day without being captured. We were given a very rough sketch map with the coordinates for a checkpoint, which we had to reach. Once we'd arrived, an agent would turn up at first light, handing us the coordinates for our next stop and a cheese sandwich. The task was designed to re-create an escape from a warzone in which we crossed over a border.

As part of our training we had already been taught how to make shelters, start fires, clean water and devise makeshift weapons. Surviving was easy. Our biggest challenge was the Hunter Force. But, despite the high stakes, there were times when I found myself laughing hysterically, probably because of the adrenaline. At one point, we were approaching a junction on a busy road and it was obvious that we were vulnerable to capture. We made our way through a field. There were several hedges shielding us from view by any passing cars, but as we crossed it, spotlights pinged on us from all angles. We were exposed. I heard the sound of motorbikes racing our way and several barking dogs.

Instinctively I hurdled a hedge, which was around ten feet high, and sprinted into the next field, laughing my head off. The dogs and bikes were getting closer. I could hear it and I knew I was in trouble, so I jumped into a nearby stream to hide. It was freezing, but with just my head popping above the water, I watched as one of the chasing pack approached the stream bank ... and then walked right past! In a Hollywood film that dog would have picked up on my scent for sure. In real life, it wasn't bothered. Somehow I had managed to avoid capture.

That didn't save me from the Resistance to Interrogation process, though. Having completed the Survive and Evade phases we made our way back to the base in a car. That's when they sprung us: guys in balaclavas with smoke bombs and guns, in a re-enactment of a hijacking. We later re-created that same scenario for the civilians who made it to the end of *Who Dares Wins* Season One because we wanted to show how the shock of capture can be so destabilising. People are at their most vulnerable, especially if they're tired, cold and hungry. They're liable to do something rash or reveal something they shouldn't. They might even turn informant, and the shock can last anywhere from five minutes to 24 hours, depending on the individual.

Straight away I was dragged in for Tactical Questioning, an aggressive form of interrogation in which the Hunter Force tried to extract as much information from me as possible. It was aggressive and their timing was vital. If they waited too long and allowed me to acclimatise as a hostage, there was a risk I might become better adjusted to their probing. I was pinned into a corner and questions were screamed at me. To keep out of trouble I mumbled a few vague details. Hands grabbed at me and I was thrown into an enclosed environment for 36 hours. It was pitch black and cold, but there was no chance of rest. I was pushed into a stress position and my stance was changed every 20 minutes or so. At one point I stood against a wall with my hands up. The next I was kneeling or squatting. It was agony.

This routine stopped me from falling asleep. My defences were weakening, and my captors knew it, so every now and then I was dragged away for more questioning. The methods were different every time. On one occasion, I was hauled through the good cop/bad cop routine. Good Cop told me to play nice.

'Look, mate,' he said. 'This next guy's going to come in and, believe me, you don't want to get on the fucking wrong side of him. Just sign the document or confess into our camera, and then that's it, I can tell him we're done. We've got what we wanted . . . He doesn't have to go mad.'

When I refused to cooperate, Bad Cop exploded into the

room, ranting and raving. He spat at my face and broke a chair over my back. I was thrown around a bit, too. All the while I told myself it was a game. I was aware that my situation wasn't real; nobody was going to kill me. Yeah, I might become exhausted, I might get roughed up a bit, but that would be the worst of it. I wasn't going to die. But around me, I could see people dropping like flies. One guy blabbed during questioning and was thrown off the course. Another was put into a room and subjected to a barrage of white noise at full blast. He was eventually taken away, screaming. There would be no room for weakness, not if anyone was to survive as a working member of the SAS.

FOXY: The Survive, Evade, Resist and Extract Phase was a giggle, but it seemed to summarise military life quite neatly. A lot of it was dull, but occasionally the monotony would be interspersed by moments of excitement. We walked through the Welsh countryside bored out of our minds for about seven days, complaining about the rain. Suddenly we'd see the Hunter Force running at us and have to start legging it. That's when the adrenaline would spike.

Of course we cheated! One of the rules was that we weren't allowed to take food from the locals, but everyone did it, and it was regarded as par for the course, as long as you didn't get caught. I think a soldier has to be a bit cheeky to make it into the Special Forces. After all, we often take whatever means necessary to complete a mission. Thinking on our feet is a skill we all need.

I was in a five-man team, and while we were hiding out

on a farm, a little old lady invited us into her house. She gave us a table full of food: roast chicken, beef sandwiches, KitKats and fizzy drinks. I think she did it every year, and she seemed to love the drama of it. It was as if she genuinely believed she was part of the Resistance, but before we left, around midnight, she asked us where we were going.

'Oh, that woodland just over there,' I told her.

The little old lady wasn't having any of it, though.

'No, no, you can access my fields,' she said. 'I've told the Army that they're not allowed to use my land, so they won't follow you . . .'

We loved her for the generosity, but it soon bit us on the arse. Once we began legging it across her fields, all of us started throwing up. We'd developed stomach cramps. Because none of us had eaten for five days, we weren't able to digest the vast amounts of food we'd consumed and it made us bloody ill.

Life didn't get that much easier once we'd been captured. I was 'harshed'. I had people in balaclavas screaming in my face. They tried to instil fear in me, they wanted me in a state of shock, but I was able to resist. At one point, though, I smirked at one of them, I was being a smart arse, and that was a big mistake. I was taken outside, into the freezing cold air, soaked with water and left to stand outside for half an hour, handcuffed to a railing. Even though I knew that nothing really bad was going to happen to me, the fatigue and stress had a detrimental impact. I was being conditioned for what might happen, should I ever be unlucky enough to fall prisoner.

5

THE FIRST MISSION

No soldier is complete after finishing Selection; expert status is still a long way off. In fact, the learning process for a Special Forces operative only really kicks in once we've started work for real. Sure, a manual or course can give us plenty of intel, but there's no substitute for learning in the heat of a battle; hands-on experience is what defines us. Likewise, if somebody's a surgeon, firefighter or police officer: no training programme can replicate the stresses and challenges of a real-life emergency – not fully.

Instead, Selection establishes a soldier as the right kind of asset, with the necessary physical and mental qualities to succeed at the highest level. Essentially, after the final stages we're viewed as a ready-made product, one that's able to adapt to a team environment immediately. But most of us only feel part of the Special Forces once a bullet has been fired at us for real.

That's when the hard work truly starts . . .

ANT: I joined the Special Boat Service in 2008 and I was often involved in missions that went noisy, sometimes from the minute we'd hit the ground. Grenades were thrown about; bullets came at us from all angles as we approached buildings and targets, but once the first round had hissed past me my training would kick in and everything slowed down. As a Special Forces operator, I had supreme confidence in myself. That came from experience. I was putting my life on the line, but I didn't feel any fear because my training had given me so much self-belief. It coursed through me.

I often felt as if I could kick in the door of an enemy compound and survive, no matter what was thrown at me. Even if enemy gunmen had their AK-47s raised, I could kill all of them before they popped off a round. I had so much confidence I remember once telling a friend of mine that I could actually *dodge* a bullet.

'I can pre-empt it,' I said. 'I know when someone's going to pull that trigger . . . And I can slow everything down.'

That must have sounded mad, but training had fine-tuned me so effectively that I could operate almost on autopilot. I understood my capabilities as a Special Forces soldier in the field of combat.

There were times, during a battle, for example, when I could have put the drop on somebody there and then, without them knowing I was there, but I often controlled my adrenaline. I had every right to shoot somebody if they had fired at us first, and there were times when my muzzle was trained at an oblivious enemy's head, but I didn't squeeze the trigger. Instead, I swiftly moved on to my next position. I knew if I fucked up and became bogged down in an avoidable firefight it might compromise my mission and the safety of the unit.

That realisation came with maturity and experience. I was able to make a decision on pulling the trigger based on my skill sets. For example, I could tell whether a fighter's gun had the magazine in and whether the weapon's safety catch was on. If there was no magazine, or the safety catch was on, I wasn't going to drop an enemy fighter for the sake of it. But if somebody was pointing a loaded weapon and the safety catch was off? You bet I'd fire first. No question.

COLIN: The first mission I was due to go on was called-off; it was pretty anti-climactic. I had been asked to ambush a patrol convoy of armoured BMWs. The attack was being co-ordinated with a Serbian warlord just after the Balkans conflict and my job was to mallet the convoy with an M94 rocket-launcher. But as we arrived at our designated location, intel reached us that our target had already been assassinated in a hotel foyer, so our mission was aborted.

My next operation was more dramatic. It took place in 2000, when I had been placed on a Forward Air Controlling

Course, a programme where you learn how to set up laser targeting systems. While training, I got a message on my pager. When I phoned in, I was told that a British passenger jet had been hijacked.

'The plane is landing shortly,' they explained. 'Can you be there for its arrival? You're going to be the first guy there . . .'

They weren't kidding. When I got to the airport, I was greeted at the front gate by the local head of police. He didn't have a clue what was happening, and when he asked how I thought we should organise ourselves, I felt a little over-whelmed.

'Oh, my God,' I thought. 'I've never run an operation of this size on my own, I didn't expect to *really* be the first guy here.'

Then my training kicked in. I understood that everybody was counting on me to hold the fort until more forces could arrive. If the shit hit the fan, I would have to storm the plane alone. I'd have had no choice. I was the only person on the ground.

'OK, I would position the police in several key areas,' I told him. 'I would get snipers, interpreters, too. We'll need to be prepared to take a lot of hostages quickly. I want to clear the surrounding area of non-essential personnel, because there's going to be press and TV media.'

Everything was happening so fast.

I was a sniper. I positioned myself near the back of the plane, where I kept watch for six hours before another Special Forces soldier arrived to relieve me. While waiting, I picked up the details of what was happening. A group of terrorists had taken the plane. The siege eventually lasted for four days, but in the end the hijackers surrendered without a bullet being fired.

FOXY: I thought my first ever mission was going to be boring, routine. We were in Afghanistan. I'd been told not to expect anything much once we'd been posted to scout out a compound in the middle of nowhere. It had been a long day. The weather was stifling and we hadn't achieved an awful lot. We were working with local forces, some trained-up Iraqi soldiers, but nothing was going on. I had itchy feet.

'Fucking hell,' I thought. 'I joined the Special Forces for action. I'm gagging to get into some sort of crazy battle. I've got all these cool weapons and stuff, but nothing's happening . . .'

I remember turning to this soldier, another Brit, and sighing loudly. He laughed.

'Yeah, Foxy. This *is* bloody boring.'

And then it all went pear-shaped.

A pickup truck flew around the corner. Hanging from the back were a bunch of militiamen, all of them aiming rifles our way. Rounds started going off, left, right and centre, and two blokes, one either side of me, were dropped – *critically injured*. How they missed me I don't know. It must have been a sheer fluke, and as I ducked for cover, my mindset changed completely.

Actually, maybe I was quite happy with being bored, sitting in a courtyard, not really doing too much . . .

Once we'd regrouped, my unit focused its fire on the militia troops shooting at us. We pushed them back, and before too long our attackers had turned on their heels, which was when we followed in pursuit, taking them out one by one. I couldn't believe it. We'd got ourselves caught up in a messy situation, quite a distance from any other Coalition assistance, and had somehow managed to scrap our way out, alone. It had been fun. I remember the adrenaline buzzing through me. I was on a high, but that was unsettling. I remember thinking, 'I enjoyed it . . . What's that all about?'

I soon became addicted to the excitement once I'd settled into life in the Special Forces. I don't know why, I don't know where it came from, but I knew it wasn't a good thing, not in my line of work. Yet I still craved it. I was like an adrenaline junkie: I loved the fact that I was living on the edge and was part of something *important*. I think that's the thing for a lot of people in the armed forces: there's a brotherhood; there's kudos for serving your country and achieving something. On the other side, there's 'the Fear'. We're all scared at one time or another, and there were times when that emotion was almost too much to handle.

One time I was involved in a hostage rescue and our helicopter had taken some heavy fire. We quickly landed, bullets were ricocheting all over the shop, and I ran out of the back, jumping into a ditch for cover. Tracer fire zinged overhead. I could hear bullets whipping past. And that's when I had a bit of a moment. I was terrified. For a split second, I wanted to go back to being a ten-year-old. I pictured a younger me, sitting with my mum, and I wanted to cry.

I soon pulled myself together and began shooting back.

Once the shit show was over and the adrenaline had died down, I wanted more. I wanted to feel like I was in a brotherhood again, fighting alongside the best, meaning something to the people working around me, whether they were my best mates or not.

It helped that I thought we were doing the right thing all of the time, even when I'd shot people. In my mind we were preventing our enemies from accessing an area from which to operate, or where they could learn new tactics. I was denying them the opportunity to come to my country, where they might plan to kill my family and my children. After a while, though, it got too much.

'Bloody hell,' I thought. 'I've rinsed myself doing this. I've given everything to keep myself going. Now I'm fucked . . .'

That's when I was told my work was done; I had finished my career with the Special Forces.

At the time I thought it was a good thing. I can't tell you the amount of times I craved for the mundane when I was on tour. During a firefight or a particularly ugly situation, I found that thinking about the smaller things in life could get me through. I drew comfort from the thought of cleaning up the house or getting nagged by my girlfriend; mowing the lawn or being dragged through a shopping centre. Once I'd returned to normality all of that was great, but within a month I was bored of being back home.

I needed that adrenaline fix again.

There were sacrifices, though. I married and divorced twice; I suffered from post-traumatic-stress disorder.

Completing so many tours of Afghanistan had burned me out and I later shut myself away. I first realised I had got myself into a bad place when a doctor asked me to think back to when my stressful episodes had first started. I couldn't remember. For six years, somebody had fired a gun at me.

Every single night.

PART TWO
MISSION PLANNING

INTRODUCTION

When executing a mission or getting the job done, there are many similarities between the civilian world and the British Special Forces – theoretically at least. Sure, our operations involve higher risks, including death or capture. However, a route map from A to B, the path that takes us from the beginning of a mission to its successful conclusion, tends to be similar to many projects and practices in a non-military environment.

In this section we'll detail the battle-tested techniques used by Special Forces units during the planning, execution and analysis (or debrief) phases of an operation. By understanding our organisational processes, you'll come to create and perfect a working formula that suits you, no matter what your role in life . . .

FOXY: Every SAS operation begins with a planning phase and ends with the debrief session. There are risks inherent in a lot of the strategies we take on, and each plan has the potential to be shot down in flames if an unexpected development strikes. But we could easily apply that description to just about any job or project undertaken by a team in any workplace. Meanwhile, as soldiers we face similar challenges to those experienced by civilian leaders. The processes aren't too different; it's just the circumstances that are amplified.

Let me explain . . .

1. WE'RE MEASURED BY OUR PERFORMANCES

Every day in life, we're judged. If we don't meet a deadline – we're screwed. If we fail to motivate ourselves, and others – we're screwed. If we're unable to hit certain targets – *screwed*. It was the same for me during my time in the military, though my parameters were very different. In the Special Forces, a mission wasn't necessarily considered a failure if a soldier died or if we suffered casualties. But if, for instance, we'd failed to capture our target in an operation or retrieve the civilians in a hostage extraction, then serious questions would have been asked afterwards.

Our successes define us, while our biggest failures can live long in the memory. In 1980, one of the Special Forces' most famous missions was a raid on the Iranian Embassy in London, when an Iranian-Arab group took 26 hostages at gunpoint and demanded the release of several Arab prisoners from the Khuzestan Province in Iran. A six-day siege ensued. On the final day, the gunmen executed a hostage, pushing his body onto the embassy steps. That's when the SAS swooped in, killing five of the six terrorists and saving all of the hostages, bar one. In the weeks and months that followed, that one mission was replayed on news shows all around the world. For years afterwards, countless documentaries investigated its success.

The images of several SAS guys dressed in black and wearing gas masks while storming the building in a cloud of smoke created some amazing, iconic photos. The papers loved it, as did the British public, and it would later inspire a film – *Who Dares Wins*, which featured the 1980s action star Lewis Collins. But imagine if the mission had been a cock-up and all the hostages had been executed? That very high-profile failure would have damaged, for a long time, too, how the SAS was perceived around the world.

As with civilian missions, results count for a lot in the Special Forces.

2. KEY DECISIONS ARE MADE UNDER DURESS . . . AND SOMETIMES CARRY UNPLEASANT CONSEQUENCES

As leaders, we often have to take action under pressure, in work or at home. Mistakes can be made. Our decisions can negatively affect others if we're not careful, and we have to live with the results. Likewise the Special Forces, though it's our job to exert extreme violence in a controlled manner, rather than dealing with an angry customer or a screwed-up project.

I've been in a number of positions where I've had to make a snap decision, usually when someone has approached me in a contact situation. In a split second I've had to assess whether that person is armed and if it's their intention to either shoot or otherwise endanger the mission. If the answer to one of those questions is 'Yes', then it's my job to fire first.

Those choices are rarely made easily, and some of them have entailed serious personal consequences. One time in Afghanistan, I was working at close quarters through a village under the cover of darkness. I was part of a team tasked with finding a Taliban leader on a high-threat detention mission. When we walked through the door of his house, I clocked somebody moving towards me. My night vision goggles were on, which created a surreal working environment, so I had to make an instant decision using very the very limited stimulus available – blurred sight, smell, hearing and touch. I instantly assessed his body language and how he was moving. There was no way he could see me. But then I saw the automatic rifle.

'Shoot,' I thought.

I squeezed the trigger. He dropped to the floor.

I turned around to check the room and that's when I noticed the kids. Three of them had been standing in a corner. Through the green tint of the NVGs I could see the awful deadpan and unemotional look that always trails shock. At the time it didn't bother me. I thought, 'Well, that's just part and parcel of what we have to deal with.' But after the mission, when time had slowed down, I ended up reflecting on the kill. I kept seeing the faces of those kids; they made me think of my own family and of how I wanted to maintain their innocence for as long as was practically possible. The lives of those children in Afghanistan had been shattered because I had made a snap decision. It caused me to struggle emotionally, even though it had been my job to shoot that guy.

Yeah, it's an extreme case study. But everyday decisions can lead to emotional blowback, too, especially if they have negative consequences for the people around us. Consider the financial decision that leads to dozens of people losing their jobs and personal security, for example.

3. WE HAVE TO ADAPT TO AN EVER-CHANGING TERRAIN . . .

In life, change happens all the time. It might be that we have a new team to work with or a new boss; we might be learning a tricky operational routine in the office or, on a basic level, negotiating a different commute to work. These are challenges that we have to adapt to, and quickly, if we're to lead to the best of our ability. Think of new terrain as technology, environments or even people. How often during our lives are we thrust into situations that make us feel uncomfortable or push us to our limits? The emotions of change can be quite a burden for most people. (And if that's not happening to you, I'd suggest you're spending too much time operating within your comfort zone.)

One of the key assets of any Special Forces soldier is

his ability to adapt to a variety of different environments. I was in the Special Boat Service and the ability to adapt was one of the biggest parts of our day-to-day job. On some missions we would start on a boat and land on a beach. From there we could move into the jungle or onto mountains. During other attacks we would dive onto a ship from a helicopter and then engage in combat on the deck or down below.

As in civilian life, it was important to remain flexible at all times. Being freaked out by change is never a good thing, and dealing with it became second nature to me.

4. . . . AND AN EVER-CHANGING ENEMY

Any competitive environment brings conflict. Rival companies go to war over new business. Industries come under threat from new technology. Individuals find their position under attack from new employees, eager to take their spot. It's vital we deal with these evolving adversaries if we're to remain secure. The failure to adapt can result in unsettling circumstances.

My personal experience of dealing with an evolving enemy is probably best summed up by several tours in Afghanistan. Our enemy, the Taliban, were not stupid. In fact, they were experts in adapting. While we were on the ground, they learned from our techniques and technology and changed their tactics accordingly. That put the onus on us to adapt to *their* methods, so we could retain *our* tactical superiority.

For instance, once the Taliban got wind that an area was suitable for a chopper landing, they made sure we would never use it again. They planted IEDs or ambushed us once we'd touched down. It took a few disastrous incidents and a number of lost lives before we learned that when flying a helicopter mission it was unwise to land in the same place twice: we had to rethink our strategy, because they had rethought theirs.

5. WE OPERATE IN MULTIFUNCTIONAL TEAMS

Any office or working environment is a mixture of different skill sets. There might be accountants, IT technicians, lawyers, human resources staff, company directors, secretaries and cleaners all operating under one roof. Overall it's their function to make sure that the company operates as effectively as possible.

I worked in units that were set up in a similar fashion. On Special Forces operations, a team would be put together depending on what was needed for a particular mission. Every soldier was part of an elite in terms of combat skills, but they would all have specialist attributes as well – during my career I was a demolitions expert, a dog handler and a combat diver.

Whatever the mission, there would always be a patrol medic, whose job was to deal with any casualties. Those guys were so experienced that they were able to walk into any hospital after their military career was finished and pick up a job. Beyond that, everybody else was selected because their particular specialty was required for the mission ahead.

THE INTEL

When planning any project, we face a range of challenges:

> Performance and results
> The consequences of decision-making
> Changing circumstances
> Changing obstacles
> Operating within a multifunctional team

As Special Forces soldiers our brains are hard-wired to work in the toughest environments. And while the tests we face are generally more unpredictable, dangerous and chaotic than any civilian project, our successful modus operandi (and skills at working out a back-up plan, should the bullets start to fly) can be applied to just about any walk of life, regardless of who we are or what we do.

If you don't believe me, apply the above principles to the role of a new parent.

> Performance and results: *just how good are we at caring for our baby?*
> The consequences of decision-making: *how will it affect our kid if we make a mistake?*
> Changing circumstances: *how do we adapt to caring for our children in a variety of circumstances – at home, in the shops, at social functions or on a family holiday?*

Changing obstacles: *how do we function when something goes wrong, such as an illness or financial change at home?*

Operating within a multifunctional team: *how do we work with our partner, family and other support groups? And can we operate more effectively together?*

All of us have missions of our own.

All of us can learn from the Special Forces.

6

THE MISSION SUCCESS CYCLE

Fail to prepare, prepare to fail: it's a cliché because it's true. This saying is particularly applicable to the Special Forces, where every mission is planned as effectively as possible – according to the time and intelligence available to us, of course. Unless we were seriously pressed for time, we wouldn't consider landing on an enemy target without first checking on the layout of the building, the capability of the enemy inside and the escape routes available. Nor should you approach any project ahead of you without a considered plan of action.

In this step-by-step chapter we'll detail how to plan out any type of mission, and prepare for the challenges and threats ahead while learning from your experiences during the delivery process. Following our cues will help you to learn and grow with every challenge. Failure to do so might lead to one hell of a screw-up . . .

OLLIE: Whatever the task, our operations in the Special Forces followed what was known as 'the Mission Success Cycle', a simple process that comprised four distinct phases:

Plan
Brief
Deliver
Debrief

This structure is applied to every mission undertaken. Sure, it looks like a very basic formula on paper, but its simplicity was deliberate because the Mission Success Cycle was designed to process large chunks of complex information in a very manageable, effective and time-efficient manner. It worked, too.

The process was also transferrable to just about every situation imaginable – hostage rescues, drugs raids or surveillance operations. That's why the Mission Success Cycle is so useful in the civilian world: this simple exercise can be applied to any working situation just as effectively. It can also be as simple or as complex as time allows.

But how?

STAGE ONE: PLAN

Let me walk you through the set-up of a hypothetical Special Forces operation. Yes, the scenario is probably very different to your working environment, but you'll soon notice that the general principles are identical. For starters, most operations usually start in a briefing area, where we work on the planning phase. As in any Mission Success Cycle, our initial step was always to determine the objective: what exactly were we trying to achieve? It was also vital for our Head of Department to outline several key issues, such as the threats we might face along the way – enemy fighters or IEDs, for example.

From there, the experience and expertise of our available personnel were evaluated. We decided who was best suited to the task before working out a plan of action. Finally, an Immediate Action plan, or IA, was settled upon. We'll talk in detail about the importance of an IA in Chapter 12, but, for now, consider it as a worst-case scenario measure, in place for when any trouble hits. Say, if we found ourselves in an impossible situation, where perhaps our targets were more heavily armed than expected and able to put up a sustained defence.

THE INTEL

The next time you're tasked with a project of any kind, at work or at home, try running through the planning process in the following order:

1. Determine your mission

What exactly are you planning to do? Outline your aims clearly. *So, for example, imagine you're the leader of a team instructed with finding a new office space for your company. Detail exactly the type of building you need to secure, the number of rooms, location and ideal amenities nearby. When are you required to move by? And, importantly, what is the company budget?*

2. Identify the threats

What problems might trouble you along the way? *It could be that the company is taking a financial risk by undertaking a move at this time. Maybe you and your team's resources will become stretched while searching for a new location. (For example, how much time can you sensibly dedicate to the project without it having a negative impact on other areas of your work?) And what type of upheavals can you expect during the process? Examine the potential dangers and work out how best to nullify them.*

3. Understand your available resources

What assets are available to you – financial, physical, and intellectual? How best can you use them? *In this case, how* much money does the company have? Do you have a detailed checklist of its locational requirements? What about time? And what research assets are at your disposal, such as estate agents, online searches or word-of-mouth intelligence?

4. Evaluate previous experiences

What happened when you last undertook a search of this kind? What worked and what didn't? In what areas did your team thrive and where did they underperform? Learn from your lessons and make time for the areas where you might be weakest. Apply the best people to the roles most suited to them.

5. Determine the best course of action

How are you going to execute your plan? When will the company's finances be in order? Which estate agents are you going to contact and when? On what days will you be available to view properties? When will you have to move by? Have a clear plan of action: who will be doing what, and when?

STAGE TWO: BRIEF

All four aspects of the Mission Success Cycle are equally important to the Special Forces during operations, but success really stemmed from the Briefing Phase.

We always readied our kit while our instructions were being delivered in a clear, concise and constructive fashion. We were then told whether the operation was 'viable'; in other words, that our chances of success were high. (I had previously gone on 'suicide missions' – attacks that carried a high chance of death, where the risk of casualties was outweighed by the gravity of the situation.) Meanwhile, any sources of confusion or conflict were ironed out in a team discussion. My experience was that establishing those details prevented procrastination from creeping in: knowledge breeds confidence, which is what enables an operation to run effectively. That's why during a Special Forces briefing *everybody involved in the Delivery Phase has to be present*. No excuses. With the briefing completed, each member of the unit knew where they were set to be, what was expected of them and what their teammates were doing.

THE INTEL

If you've decided to deliver a brief (and when operating in a team environment, this is a priority), ask the following questions before opening your mouth.

- Is what you're about to say clear, concise and constructive?
- Is everybody involved in the mission present in the room? And do they fully understand what's expected of them?
- Is what you're about to present viable? In a military sense, this means a mission can be completed without the risk of large casualties. In civilian terms, a viable operation is one that doesn't create a heavy drain on resources,

reputation or morale. If what you're presenting isn't viable, *warn your team*.

STAGE 3: DELIVER

The business end of any operation. If the planning and briefing stages have been completed properly, and everybody performs their tasks expertly, this phase should be a success, though not always. We have a saying in the Special Forces that 'No plan survives first contact.' Basically, it's our way of recognizing that tactics and detailed briefings often fly out of the window once we've encountered the enemy, especially if a situation goes noisy. Hopefully, that won't be the case for you.

THE INTEL

If you've done your Planning and Briefing Phases correctly, you should be able to complete your mission effectively, with everybody in your team engaged in the project once the call to action has been made. REMEMBER: *'No plan survives first contact.'* Be prepared for mistakes and worst-case scenarios, especially if one of your predetermined threats comes into play.

STAGE 4: DEBRIEF

You'll be surprised at just how many teams, companies and organisations tend to sidestep the debriefing process once a project has been completed. However, this procedure is a vital element of the Mission Success Cycle. Why? Well, for starters, it presents everybody with the opportunity to learn and improve, regardless of whether the operation has been a success or not. Meanwhile, vital intelligence can be shared between different teams, and maybe across entire organisations, especially when studying the broader picture of an ever-changing enemy.

In the Special Forces, we tend to debrief almost from the minute we've rolled back into base. The meeting is always held in a group setting, and each team involved explains their role and what took place during the Delivery Phase. From there, any problems that were encountered are discussed, as are the positive aspects of the mission. But one of the most important aspects of a Special Forces debrief is the removal of hierarchy: rank becomes obsolete; everybody's opinions are valid, and the session is an open forum where anyone can express their concerns, experiences and ideas.

The Special Forces are quite unique in that respect. For too long, the British Army, or what we call the 'Green Army', has been hung up on the idea of hierarchy. Everybody has a rank, everybody interacts accordingly, but that doesn't cut it with us. That's because everybody in the Special Forces is expected to be a leader *and* a team player, and each of us is considered to be on the same level. I've seen Green Army officers make their way into the SAS or SBS. Initially they've tried to stamp their authority on a group, but it doesn't take long before somebody has given them a slap or told them to shut up. A superior attitude doesn't wash with us.

This idea of rank and file also extends to the civilian world, where companies or team environments have a clear pecking order of authority. Usually, what's being communicated from the top is deemed more valid than what's said lower down; people without authority feel scared to speak up. But that kind of environment is, at best, a waste of resources. At the very worst, it can be risky. Anybody at any level can come up with a great plan or stumble across a vital piece of intelligence. If we were to ignore anybody below the rank of team leader in the Special Forces, then we might miss out on vital information, something that might be the difference between blowing a mission and saving hundreds, if not thousands, of lives. Meanwhile, it's vital that we create an environment where individuals can feel comfortable when expressing an opinion or idea. We want our team members to think for themselves, and to take initiative, rather than blindly following orders from above. It's a sure way of developing future leaders.

THE INTEL

Once a project has been completed, hold a debrief session as soon as possible, regardless of whether it's been a success or a failure. If the delivery phase does not go to plan, regroup, debrief and – next time – rebrief.

- Your meeting should take place without rank. Everybody is capable of spotting a game-changing piece of information, regardless of position and experience. Unless we listen to the comments of everyone within our team – and at every level – it's impossible to build a 360-degree view of what has happened. *If, say, a supermarket was looking to improve the functionality of the store, why would management restrict an ideas session to just the senior members of staff? The workers on the shop floor – not to mention the security guards and trolley collectors – are their boots on the ground. Generally, they'll speak to customers on a daily basis. As an information resource, they will have a first-hand picture of what works well and what doesn't.*

- Make sure any key information that emerges from the debrief is shared within the team. Your team might be working on several projects at once. One piece of information gleaned from your work might affect all of them.
- If you work alone, conduct a personal debrief. Just make a series of notes that can be referred back to the next time you work on a similar project. You never know when it might provide a key piece of intel. Likewise, what methods and techniques worked and failed during the mission? By analysing the successes and failures within a Delivery Phase we can learn valuable lessons and improve our future working methods.

7

THE ART OF
TACTICAL BRIEFING

It's one thing to work through a detailed and thoroughly researched Planning Phase. It's an entirely different matter when it comes to successfully delivering orders to the people around you, especially when a ton of intel is flying around, and the pressure is great. Info can become confused; people lose sight of their responsibilities.

We touched upon the importance of briefing in the previous chapter, but there's so much more to this process than simply laying down a series of orders. The instructions must be well planned and thought out. Meanwhile, clear communication is key. A team leader can arrive at a meeting with the best-laid plans in mind, yet because the information hasn't been organised in a coherent fashion, their requests become muddled. Their colleagues can feel confused; a project gets off to a shoddy start.

The Special Forces work differently. Once the Planning Phase is completed, we move into a Briefing stage and it's here that high-threat operations are laid out in a clear and concise fashion. This chapter details some of the methods used in the theatre of combat to avoid miscommunication and disorder.

ANT: A Special Forces soldier is always forward-thinking – he looks to the future, rather than dwelling on the past – and for one simple reason: whenever an operation goes wrong, with forward thinking we're still good. We can adapt. *We can still perform.* And, believe me, things *do* go wrong, probably 90 per cent of the time, in fact.

Ollie previously detailed the belief that, '*No plan survives first contact.*' But it's not just a burst of enemy fire or a dead teammate that can cause problems; other factors come into play, too. Like inaccurate intel, for example, or plain old bad luck. We might land on a terrorist camp expecting to capture a key figure for interrogation, only to discover the enemy evacuated minutes earlier. In an instant, the mission has changed, but rather than flying back to the base in a sulk, we move into a different operation – information gathering, say. The place is then raided for site-sensitive equipment, such as SIM cards, mobile phones, guns and laptops. The Special Forces won't allow an unfortunate issue to derail us. We accept a problem and immediately move into a different operation.

That attitude is partly to do with our personalities, and partly to do with our training. But it also comes from the briefing process. During the Planning Phase on every mission we discuss what might go wrong. Within the briefing session, we then explain what to do if those issues come into play. That's why this component of the Mission Success Cycle is so important, and why everybody should implement it in their working practices. During my time in the military it was often the difference between our turning a negative outcome to our advantage and allowing it to defeat us.

Delivering an effective brief isn't easy, though. You have to understand all the intelligence available before detailing a mission or objective to a team of people willing to work for you. Just as important is how you absorb the information if you're the one being briefed. It's here that everybody can learn one or two tricks from the Special Forces.

THE TARGET PACK

While serving on a tour of Afghanistan with the Special Forces, I was involved in multiple high-threat detention missions. Our targets were usually Taliban members operating on the Pakistan border. Some of them were commanders, others were IED facilitators, weapon distributors and cash facilitators who operated within certain provinces in Afghanistan. They would cross back and forth every couple of months to resupply their troops or get a heads-up on what was going on in Afghanistan. Most of the time, these guys would stay in what they thought was a safe location for a couple of days before heading back over the border, which is where we scooped them up, usually for interrogation. However, if the worst came to the worst, and it looked as if our target was heavily protected, more drastic measures were taken.

During the Briefing Phase, each operative of would be given a Target Pack – a file containing all the important details on our man. Every piece of relevant intel could be found inside: there was a photo or two, usually satellite shots; we would read details of who he was and what responsibilities he held; which places he frequented and with whom. Was there a risk of collateral damage during our attack? Was he travelling with women and children? And, could he potentially pose a threat to us during the mission? All of this information was detailed thoroughly, and as quickly as possible

Then there were the logistical details of our mission, namely how we were going to attack and where we were due to be extracted from afterwards. This would give us a clear idea of how the mission should pan out and what equipment was needed, as well as a time frame. Sometimes the airspace above us was restricted for a short period of time, allowing us to get in and out without encountering another mission. Those windows also allowed air support to fly in quickly and effectively. Beyond that, we were considered adults, trusted to think for ourselves. We had been trained in what it was we had to do and how to do it. We didn't need any more specifics.

Besides, overloading an operative with too much info could be counterproductive at any level and on any job. *So, for example, it could be that you're taking your team to meet a prospective client. In which case, do give them the vital details on their company, their requirements, and how they operate. Don't bog them down with needless background information such as an in-depth company history or an extensive list of directors.*

THE INTEL

Before any project, deliver your team their Target Pack: a well-ordered file of information that presents them with a clear idea of what's expected, both as a group and individually. But remember:

- State the objective clearly. *Say the company you work for has asked your team to pitch to an individual for business. Before giving your staff the details of the job in hand, create your own Target Pack explaining exactly what your potential customer is looking for and how you can present yourselves as the best choice. What are the deal-breakers that can bring you success?*
- Keep the info short and sweet. Don't bog people down in too many facts, as it can become counterproductive.
- Trust your team to know their job. Don't patronise them or overburden them with basic details they already know – they will only lose focus.

- If you're the one being briefed, make sure you understand the objectives, and always, *always*, ask questions if there's something you're unsure of.

The Orders Process

The Orders Process is the Commanding Officer's instructions, and the brief for a high-threat detention mission will run along these lines:

'Lads, let's keep it simple. I won't baffle you with too much information, I don't want to overload your minds. Our target is Bravo Two. He is an IED facilitator of the Helmand Province, and he's been staying at Location A. We believe the compound is holding him and his bodyguards only. There's a sentry position here and here. Bravo Team, you're going to come in from the east. Delta Team, you're going to come in from the west. Alpha Team, it's your job to deal with the squirters* from the Sea King helicopter.

'Once the compound is deemed clear and we're all given the word "Clear!", then we'll make sure the cordon's out. From there we'll extract to Location B, where we'll be picked up by two CH-47s [Chinook helicopters] and extracted to Location Z. The extraction is five kilometres from the target, and it will take us approximately 45 minutes to get back to base. Time to mission from here is 35 minutes. Everyone clear with that?

❋   Squirters are runners, enemy forces fleeing, or 'squirting' from, a building or a location that we've been attacking.

'Everyone happy with the roles?

'Everyone happy with the summary?

'Everyone happy with the whole mission in general?'

It really is that basic. Meanwhile, each person involved in the briefing session will be encouraged to ask questions at the end – it's imperative that everybody should understand the mission from top to bottom. Miscommunication or ignorance can quite easily be the difference between success and failure, life or death. Most importantly, though, the person delivering the Orders Process must be familiar with the operation from top to bottom, so they can deliver their instructions clearly in a succinct, but thorough, speech.

It should be the same for you when delivering a briefing, or Orders Process, of your own. Understand the operation you and your team are undertaking in its entirety. Clearly state the objective of the mission and the actions required during the Delivery Phase. Then open a channel of dialogue between the team and yourself – somebody you're working with might spot an issue that's passed you by. Remember, leaving yourself open to queries is not a sign of weakness, rather an indication of strength.

Your team is an asset. Use them.

THE INTEL

Here are a few things you should ask yourself before presenting an Orders Process:

- Do you understand the mission completely? *Or, following on from the example used earlier, have you done your research on the company you're about to pitch to? Do you know its key requirements and how best you can deliver them? Do you know the basic information on deadlines, dates and personnel requirements?*
- Is the information you're about to deliver as clear and succinct as possible? *Have you detailed your plan of action in a succinct and digestible format?*
- Are you prepared to answer any questions your team might want to throw at you? If the answer is 'No', I suggest you return to your research. A complete understanding of the mission will give you the strongest sense of authority.

One thing to note here: not everybody will agree with you. I've been on missions where I've been unsure of the outcome, even my survival, because of certain risk factors, uncertain intelligence and so on. That's when I've asked questions. I've always followed through with the orders because (a) I respected the Commanding Officer and (b) I respected the CO's Orders Process. If the brief is well planned, your mission should be executed accordingly.

Brief from experience; lead from the front

Good leadership – in any situation – isn't simply about dishing out orders in the Briefing Phase. It's about setting an example, too. Look at some of the great team captains in sport. It's not enough for them to simply bark orders or yell like a madman. They lead by working hard. It's the same in the SAS or SBS. People have been happy to take instructions from me because I've been the point man on too many missions to count – I've been the first through a door when death could have been waiting for me on the other side. Good leaders get their hands dirty.

My advice to anyone struggling to inspire respect during the Briefing Phase would be to take on one of the tougher tasks on the list, or at least be on hand to deliver advice. *If we were to continue the example of our hypothetical pitch, maybe take on one of the more pressurised or labour-intensive roles during the research stages. Show the team that you're willing to roll up your sleeves, too. It can reap serious benefits in the long run.*

Use the Briefing Phase to show you have experience. *Command respect.*

8

HOW TO COMMUNICATE EFFECTIVELY

Some people seem to thrive at the front of a crowded meeting room. They can deliver clear instructions and engage their teammates with ease. Those people are in the minority, however. For most of us, delivering important instructions to a group of colleagues can tear us out of our comfort zone. One mistake or misstep leaves us exposed and open to judgement or criticism.

A Special Forces soldier doesn't have time for such psychological hang-ups. When issuing instructions, it's our job to speak clearly and concisely. That's not to say there aren't subtle nuances that can be gleaned from our methods of communication. We rarely bark out orders and expect everybody to follow them, no questions asked. Instead, the way in which we deliver instructions is the glue that binds a mission together; we can identify tactical strengths and responsibilities. Problems and weaknesses can be headed off at the pass. And sometimes we learn something about a teammate that might just help us later down the line.

PART 1. THE POWER OF WARM AND COLD COMMANDS

ANT: It's not enough to bark out a series of orders and then wait for the results to roll in. As leaders, in and out of the Special Forces, we can all learn from our instructions. I'm not talking about our distribution of intelligence or operational details, but rather about how the team responds to operational requests. And you can tell a lot about a soldier depending on what questions they ask following an expertly delivered brief, as well as how they respond to difficult challenges.

I describe instructions in one of two ways – they can be either cold or warm. A cold instruction is always straightforward and to the point; there's nothing in the way of extra detail. In civilian terms that could be, 'Set up a meeting with Company X.' Or, to give you a Special Forces example, 'Secure the compound.' On paper, both mission objectives *sound* as if they might be fairly basic tasks, but only if the people working towards them are familiar with the relevant details, such as the contact details for Company X or the safest way of entering the compound without taking a bullet. That's why a team leader should only give out cold commands if they're 100 per cent certain that the people they've instructed are in possession of all the vital details or are suitably experienced. If we don't, one of two things will happen. (Though we can learn a lot about the individuals we're working with from both.)

1. The team, or individual, will bombard us with a million questions. That might seem annoying at first but, ultimately, it's a good thing. Why? Well, their questions reveal a willingness to complete the mission effectively, regardless of what we may, or may not, think of them.

2. The team, or individual, muddles through, hoping to get everything right without making an almighty cock-up. Of course, this is less annoying for us in the short term, though it could lead to a potentially disastrous situation later on.

A warm command is very different, however. It arrives with detail, and clear instructions. So, to return to the example of our team opening up lines of communication with Company X, good leaders will suggest several points of contact – phone numbers, email addresses and so on. When ordering their troops to secure an enemy compound, the Special Forces team leader will present all the intelligence available to them at that moment – the number of enemy soldiers on the ground, best entry points to the building, extraction details and so on.

In an ideal world, what happens next is this: our teams nail the delivery with little or no fuss. Following a warm command, one or two questions are understandable. However, if you've delivered a detailed Target Pack and strong Orders Process, any more than one or two might suggest a team hasn't been listening. Likewise, if there has been very little in the way of enquiries or feedback and your team screws up the Delivery Phase big style, then it hints at poor discipline, a team or individual that can't be arsed, or a lack of focus. Nobody wants those flaws on their team when the stakes are seriously high.

PART 2. THE IMPORTANCE OF SPEAKING OUT

OLLIE: Speaking up and expressing opinions, doubts and ideas, in or out of the Briefing Phase, always counts for something. Meanwhile, keeping your mouth shut can sometimes lead to regrets. I know this from personal experience: *the one time I didn't voice my concerns, it cost a man his life.* It's a mistake I now regard as the biggest of my military career.

It happened in Baghdad, just after the fall of Saddam Hussein in 2003. The war had ended, or so we thought. In reality, the conflict was only just beginning and there was a false sense of security about the place. Behind the scenes, militia groups were preparing to start their guerrilla campaign, not that we knew, and at times I would drive through the city alone with just a concealed pistol stuffed down my trousers. That's how unconcerned I was about the situation.

One night, a guy we were working with told us he was going to a party in a hostile section of the city. I knew he could handle himself — he was in the SBS — but there was a part of me that worried about his attitude. I had been watching him for the past few months and noticed that he had become 'localised'; he had gone rogue. By that I mean he was moving into the Iraqi lifestyle. He was seeing a girl from Baghdad, and he had grown his hair long, which was complemented by a big beard. It was as if he thought he had become part of the local community.

We were due to fly out the following day for another mission, so I didn't say anything to him — I figured he would have his fun and we would all be on the plane together the next day. This guy was also a strong character, there was a lot of experience on his CV. He commanded respect, so everybody in the team was almost scared to even broach the subject with him. What we should have said was, 'Look, mate, you shouldn't go. It's too risky.' Instead, we kept our mouths shut. When we arrived at the airport the following morning, he was a no-show. The next thing we heard, he had been found murdered.

I should have trusted my instincts; I should have said something, but, instead, I opted for an easier life and decided not to have a difficult conversation with someone who probably would have reacted badly. Never again, though. After the tragedy, I made a promise to myself that if I had something to say, I would air my opinion, regardless of intimidation or fear. Had I spoken up back then, he might still be alive. Then again, it might not have changed his mind. He might still have been murdered that night, but at least I would have tried.

PART 3. BUILD YOUR OWN GREATEST HITS

ANT: Communication doesn't come easily to everyone. Inspiring people to do their best for us can seem tricky at times, especially if we're just getting used to a new role or an increased level of responsibility. I felt that way when I first moved into the Special Forces, but I learned everything I could about giving and receiving orders by watching the people around me during team meetings and the Orders Process.

During my first tour of Afghanistan when I was with the SBS, I watched how the senior guys (the team leaders) delivered their briefs; I studied how they organised their Target Packs. I would then see how the other operatives took on their orders and asked questions. Once I'd figured out how the better soldiers organised their kits and weapon systems, I copied them. As soon as I got the opportunity, I would mimic their techniques on the range. I was always trying to better myself.

I wasn't naïve. I didn't know everything, and so at every given opportunity I would soak up information like a sponge. I loved putting myself into situations where I felt I could learn something. If my team was sitting around, drinking wets, waiting for our next operation to kick off, and I noticed another Orders Process taking place across the base, I would excuse myself and watch what was going on. From there, I'd cherry-pick the techniques and communication methods I felt worked the most effectively. In a way, I made a Special Forces' Greatest Hits compilation and used it for my own work.

We can all learn from the people around us. And there's no harm in watching and learning from the very best, no matter what field we operate in.

THE INTEL

- Accept questioning as part of your role. No matter what job you do, as a leader it's your responsibility to engage with people's enquiries, especially if they're regarding the instructions they've been given by you. *Whether that be a fellow teacher expressing concerns about a syllabus, a colleague from a sports team asking about their responsibility on the pitch or a designer enquiring about a tone for their work, your engagement and clarification could save a lot of time in the long run.*

- Use your instructions as intelligence. Always note the people who ask questions and those who wander blindly into a project without enquiry. It's far better to have someone on your team who wants to understand than someone who might not really care. Also, test the mettle of a new colleague by seeing how they react to warm commands. It will teach you a lot about their work ethic.

- Always speak out. If you have a concern regarding a project or issue, mention it. Your input may have a positive outcome further down the line.

- Build your own greatest hits. Look at the people around you who do their job well. Who thrives under pressure? In your workplace, who delivers to a consistently high standard? Watch them. See how they operate. Pick their brains for intelligence. Then take the best of what they have to offer and apply it to your own game.

9
THE VALUE OF INTEL

These days, intelligence is everything and in all walks of life, too. It prepares us for how we might act in different situations or how we should plan for a certain issue. In our personal lives, it could be that we're meeting someone for the first time; knowing they've had a recent family bereavement might cause us to tread carefully during conversation. In a business setting, we might learn that a rival company is struggling financially and has become primed for takeover. Or knowing what our predecessor earned for the job we're set to take should help us during contract negotiations.

In this chapter we'll look at the value of intelligence, how to separate the good from the bad, and how best to apply it to your situation.

ANT: In the Special Forces, intel arrives from all over the place. We gather it through various sources, and it gives us a better idea of the kind of individual we're targeting, an ISIS leader, say, or a location such as a base that we need to destroy. It might even focus on an asset that we're hoping to capture or eliminate, valuable documents or a weapon stash. Most of the time, intel will come in one of several forms: technology; air and ground surveillance, or human intelligence (humint) such as an informant or prisoner.

In the civilian world, it works on a fairly similar level. Pretty much all of us have technological info at our fingertips these days with newsfeeds on Twitter or Facebook. And we might have informants (humint) of our own – someone from a rival firm who wants to leave, or a new person arriving from a different company who's willing to share their operational procedures. Holding that information might encourage us to make decisions or alter our strategies. However, when it comes to utilising intel, the difference I've found between civilian life and the Special Forces is that, in the SAS or SBS we never, ever take our data as gospel. Believe me, getting wrong intel can be as bad as, if not worse than, having none at all.

I remember one occasion in Afghanistan when we were ordered to sneak up on a Taliban compound and take out a key target. Ordinarily, we would have approached the building at night, moving in and out of the area very quickly. But on this occasion we were informed that the area surrounding the building was peppered with IEDs, meaning we had to creep through cautiously, under the cover of darkness, to mine-sweep and mark our routes in and out. It took all night, which slowed the operation down considerably, and because of the delay we ran into a two-day shit storm with enemy soldiers. Even worse, it turned out our intel was wrong. There were no IEDs. *So where the hell did they get that information?*

THE INTEL

Be prepared for your information to be wrong. And if it is inaccurate, don't let it derail you. Whenever that happened to us on missions, we still got the job done, because adaptability is a key attribute of any Special Forces soldier. We accepted our sources had been wide of the mark and moved on, but it served as a reminder to digest everything we were told and to use it carefully. No matter what job we're in, we should learn which sources of information are most trustworthy to us. *For example, a football journalist might have a tried and tested contact when it comes to gaining information on transfer deals. It makes sense that, after a period of working with that particular person, their intel will have a higher value than someone who has approached them on Twitter.*

I found it helped to prioritise my intel before missions. There is some information that is essential, some that at best is just background noise, and at worst can really trip you up. The reliable stuff I prioritised. The less reliable stuff, I looked over and parked in the back of my mind, should I need it later on. Whenever I went into the Delivery Phase, I focused on the important details. So, if I was working on a high-threat detention mission, I focused on the target and their location because that information was spot on 99.9 per cent of the time. Beyond that, I accepted the intel within our Target Packs might be a bit off. For example, I've been on missions where there were ten guards on sentry duty rather than the two we were promised.

Let me couch this prioritisation of intel in more familiar terms: the job interview. We've all had them, and at times we've been able to gather some info on the interviewer in advance. They could be a friend of a friend; maybe they sit at a desk with someone we know. It might be that we've gathered some info from Facebook about that person's background – the team they support or the bands they like, allowing us to build a profile of what kind of person they are.

In our head, the Target Pack might look something like this:

- The company is looking for someone with experience, expertise and flexibility.
- The last person in the position quit because 'the money stunk' and they were being forced to work at weekends.
- According to a mate, your interviewer likes a party; they are part of the after-work drinking crowd.
- On their list of likes on Facebook, they're vegetarian, they support Spurs and watch *Game of Thrones*; judging by their photos they got pretty wasted at Glastonbury last year.

OK, with all that intel, where do you go? My advice is: focus on the first line of data only – *the vitals*. Everything else is garnish and based on hearsay, so don't act on it. For example, it would be disastrous to ask whether there was any truth in the rumour that the last person in the job quit because they had been asked to work weekends. That said, do be prepared should some of the other intel come into play. You might get asked if you like football (don't slag off Spurs); how you fill your spare time could come up, so mention some bands you like and the TV box sets you've binge-watched recently. But before you get on to that, focus on the key details first – the job requirements.

I learned to my cost that most intel should be treated with the utmost caution. The only thing I came to expect before a mission started? Bullets were set to fly over my head as soon as I'd touched the ground.

10
PREPARING YOUR ARMOUR

A successful team is built on different attributes. It comprises a variety of strengths and weaknesses. And understanding the different variables that make up a group of people working towards the same goal can be the difference between success and failure.

For example, picture a profitable clothes store. Some members of the staff might be fantastic at buying stock and predicting market trends. Somebody else might be adept on the financial side; there are workers who will feel more comfortable working with customers on the shop floor than dealing with advertising or PR. The best businesses succeed because they understand how best to prepare their armour for the challenges ahead. Or, in other words, how to maximise the talents of their team members.

It's an idea that we've long carried into the Special Forces. In this chapter we reveal the SAS's principles of putting square pegs into square holes, managing talent, and expanding the skill sets within our soldiers. Then we'll explain how they can be applied to your life.

FOXY: Every team has unique characteristics, such as areas of expertise, personality types and levels of experience. The key to leading any group of people during a mission is to build upon their collective strengths while managing any areas of weakness. Different missions required different skill sets. When it came to mission planning our Commanding Officers had to make sure they chose the right tools for the job.

This is true in the most literal sense, too – before operations, the team leader would have an array of equipment to choose from including explosives, high-tech optical equipment, such as NVGs, and surveillance gadgets. It was important to achieve the right balance: we had to select the appropriate range of gear to cover all likely eventualities, while not carrying so much that the men were weighed down, which could potentially compromise the mission. From there, a team was assembled based on the requirements of a job. When I was in Afghanistan, one of my roles was to work as a demolitions expert. During raids, it was down to me to blow a compound wall or door, so the rest of the team could storm in. (That was much more fun than kicking a door down.*) Sometimes, I'd have to blow a whole building up. It all depended on the mission.

During my time in Afghanistan we received intel that one of the most important Taliban figures was hiding in a nearby village and our CO put together a team for a high-threat detention mission. Several teams were set to attack his compound simultaneously and each was built up of specialists required for a certain task. I was involved because there was a perimeter wall to be blown. My job was to select the right explosives, depending on the information we had received regarding the thickness of the structure and its height, as well as the material it had been built from.

Alongside me in the four-man unit was a patrol medic, just in case anybody got injured. There was also a point man, the guy charged with leading our attack. Their role varied according to the mission. Sometimes they might have to navigate a team across 15 miles of arid landscape. Other missions would involve shorter distances, such as sprinting across a courtyard or through an entry point, like a door. But their work was vital in the running of the operation, and in this case it was their role to step into the compound first, after I had blown a hole in the wall.

This wasn't a rag-tag team. Everyone had a specific

---

* One of the many things we were taught in the Special Forces was how to break through a door. Kicking it in wasn't usually the best method of attack. It all depended on where the lock had been positioned and what style of lock it was. The type of frame and materials are important, too. Believe me, I could talk about it for hours.

function within the mission; everybody knew exactly what they were supposed to be doing. We had planned. We were briefed and understood what was expected of us within the Mission Success Cycle. Confidence was high. Because of our training, all of us had a belief in ourselves, as well as the people alongside us.

As well as our specialist abilities, such as demolitions or medical, all of us were clued up in other skill sets. This was because we had been told to pick up other areas of expertise once we had moved in the Special Forces. These were called Add Quals (additional qualifications) and they often came in handy. As well as being a demolitionist and dog handler, I was also a sabotage expert and skilled in different methods of entry.

So educational courses were vital within a Special Forces unit, as was experience. I know of medics who would set themselves up on a week's detachment in a hospital A&E to prepare themselves for a tour in Afghanistan. In a way, the Special Forces end up preparing their operatives for life after their military career is over by turning them into the kind of multiskilled workers any employer would be keen to hire.

Most importantly, this broad educational process meant that every soldier was capable of thinking on the ground, in a changing environment, and able to employ a variety of different skill sets. As a military force, we were capable of preparing a team to face just about any situation or environment imaginable.

SQUARE PEGS INTO SQUARE HOLES

We advanced on the building and I blew the wall. Within moments, our point man was through the entry area and we had located the target. As a unit we had deployed the right tools at the right time and completed our task.

The nuts and bolts of our success could be found in the mission brief. It was strong. Everybody from the commander down understood exactly what needed to be done. With a clear idea of what had to be achieved we were able to assemble a group of people with an appropriate range of skill sets. Or in other words, sticking to the basic principle of putting square pegs into square holes. Too often, team leaders forget this process and they give roles according to seniority rather than ability. *For example, an important presentation might go to a staff member with status, rather than a newer face who has genuine expertise when speaking in public. On other occasions, people are just handed roles on a project without any thought being given to what their respective skill sets make them most suited to doing.*

But how should we distribute responsibility? I would recommend the Special Forces' emphasis on ignoring rank during the Planning Phase. Sometimes the most junior member of an SAS operational unit can possess the strongest skills for a mission. We should also encourage honesty. A team leader will mistakenly believe a certain member of the group is ideal for a particular role. That person might know of someone alongside them who's better suited for the project, but they're fearful about piping up. They don't want to be seen to be challenging their boss or shirking work.

In reality, they're threatening the mission. Encouraging team members to come forward and express their opinions, regardless of rank, can be a useful tool when managing our weaknesses.

MANAGE THE SKILL SETS WITHIN A TEAM

When I first became a demolitionist in the Special Forces, I had to be trained up – I didn't just walk in with a box of bombs. There were modular courses, formulas to study. I had to learn a hell of a lot of maths, not to mention a large number of sums involving measurements of explosives and wall depths. Luckily all this information was passed on to me by the Regiment's demolitions expert.

I made the most of every second with him so I could become an asset on missions. Every time we worked on deto-nations together, I watched how he did things. I soaked up his techniques. Eventually it got to a point in my Special Forces career where I was the one doing the teaching. That seemed mad to me at first, but it quickly taught me a valuable lesson about team building: everyone in the group had to be an expert in something different.

There was no use in me learning to be a demolitions man if there were ten others in the Regiment who could do the job better than me. My COs knew I was highly skilled in blowing stuff up. Therefore I was a valuable asset, and called upon every time demolitions were required. My expertise made us stronger as a team, as did the specialties of the people around me. But while there would be little point in there being 50 demolitions experts in the regiment, it would be just as disastrous to only have one medic between us. The skill sets of each individual were created to match the requirements of the Special Forces as a whole.

If we're to make our teams stronger – in any walk of life – we have to ensure there's an even spread of skills within the group. First of all, we have to work out what requirements we need as a team to operate efficiently and successfully. Then it's vital we distribute those talents accordingly, or we train certain individuals so that our resources are applied correctly. To put it in a football context: what would happen if we were to field a team of eleven centre forwards? It would get ugly; our defensive weaknesses would be exposed pretty quickly. Defeat would be inevitable.

EXPAND THE EXPERTISE

There's a lot to be learned from the Special Forces' insistence on Add Quals. Their attitude seemed to be: 'Let's teach people as much as we can, because at some point, they may need to call upon it.' It worked, too, especially when units were caught in an unexpected firefight and had to draw upon an improvised plan. My extracurricular studies on different methods of entry came in handy on a few occasions.

That expanded skill set made me more versatile, too.

During the Afghanistan war I became a dog handler, which seemed pretty crazy at the time. The Americans started doing it first of all. They were ten years down the line, and at one stage they asked the British Special Forces for some volunteers to get involved with the programme. I had no idea why I put my hand up – I think it was because it was different, but I also had a dog when I was a kid. I quite liked them, so I thought, 'Why not?'

I was taken up to a camp in Melton Mowbray for what was called an Intro to Dog Course. It was very basic, but it was the jumping-off point to one of the most interesting aspects of my career. I was paired off with a dog and together we did some crazy stuff together. He was an attack dog and a sniffer who could smell out explosives, weapons and people. It was a weird role to take on, but it expanded my horizons and I increased my opportunities as a result.

My feeling is we should encourage our team members (and ourselves) to go on new courses – creating a culture of permanent learning. No matter what our levels of experience, we should always be looking to learn new skills within our field. After all, expanding the expertise within ourselves, and our team, might reward us in unexpected ways.

THE INTEL

OK, with the above principles in mind, let's apply them to a school staff room.

- Square pegs in square holes: if the Year 10 football team needs a new, voluntary manager, ask somebody who has a passion for the game, rather than the teacher with the most spare time on their hands.
- Manage your staff's skill sets: list your team and detail their strengths and weaknesses. It might be that you're presented with an abundance of language teachers and a shortage of experienced heads of year. In which case, the next time a vacancy on your staff comes up it might be worth approaching an ambitious young teacher with ideas of eventually progressing to a head teacher role, rather than a budding French tutor.
- Expand the expertise: encourage your team and colleagues to advance their abilities by offering a range of courses outside school such as new IT skills, languages or first aid. You never now when it might come in handy.

And yeah, all of these tips might seem obvious on paper, but you'd be amazed at just how few people take notice of them in practice.

11
THE PRAYERS MEETING

How we learn from our successes and failures is what allows us to improve. And how we analyse ourselves, and the people around us, gives us the opportunity to detail our strengths and weaknesses. During Selection, every Special Forces hopeful is studied on a daily basis. Their skills are appraised by the DS; their flaws are exposed. But it's only through sharing intel amongst the assessing group that we can truly find a 360-degree view on whether a soldier has what it takes to progress.

It should be the same in the civilian world. No matter what job we're undertaking or what project we're involved in, a regular period of information sharing and analysis is vital if we're to gain strength in the future. Here's how you can implement this process – also known as the Prayers Meeting – into your working practices.

ANT: At the end of every key stage of the Selection process the Directing Staff traditionally holds the 'Prayers Meeting'*, a gathering of intelligence on the soldiers hoping to pass through to the Special Forces. Ultimately, it's an appraisal process (sometimes it's 360 degrees in style, other times not) and an opportunity to share information. During the discussion, every recruit is scrutinised, and their strengths and flaws are assessed.

Everybody's voice matters during these discussions, and what's useful in the Prayers Meeting is that the DS gets to see a soldier from all angles, and opinions on each candidate can be very different. Let's say I've been impressed by one bloke's physical and mental strength during the Hills Phase. My attitude might later change should another member of the DS inform me that the same guy lost his rag through hunger and fatigue an hour or so after I'd returned to base. That chink in his armour could ultimately be the difference between him passing through or being kicked out on his arse, because there's one question we ask of ourselves when discussing every recruit: *At*

---

*   I've heard it was first called the Prayers Meeting because it takes place in the evening, a time when many people would have been making peace with God. In the heat of battle, a lot of soldiers would have been hoping not to take a bullet the next day.

the end of the day, would I be happy with this bloke alongside me in a warzone?

During the making of *SAS: Who Dares Wins*, Season One, the DS held a Prayers Meeting nearly every night and the shared intelligence proved very useful when learning about the civilians we were working with. One candidate, Anthony Selwyn – recruit no. 27, a professional dancer – had impressed us all with his durability. He was fairly tough. However, one of the lads noticed that Anthony reacted very badly whenever he was cold and wet. I wanted to see how far Anthony could go, so that night I decided to break him.

When everybody rose for training the next day, I worked Anthony hard, making sure he worked through every river on the Sickener – an endurance run which took place on the terrain around the Brecon Beacons. This was a gruelling test of physical and mental endurance that only ended once six recruits had bailed out. (Not that we told them. As a result, it lasted several hours.) Whenever I had the opportunity, I forced Anthony to do push-ups in puddles. Almost straight away I could tell that our intelligence had been correct. Because he was a skinny lad, Anthony couldn't deal with being cold or wet. I knew it might snap him so, as the day wore on, I made him lie down in a stream for five minutes; when I told him to sprint through the sea during a beach run, I could tell he hated every second of it. But fair play to him, Anthony didn't break. He surprised us all and pushed on through.

Sometimes, though, the DS can disagree on an individual during the Prayers Meeting. In the case of an MMA fighter,

Phil Hoban, recruit no. 07, most of us believed that he wasn't up to it, as far as the Selection process was concerned. His son, Callam Charlesworth, 19 years old, no. 06, had also made it onto the show, but we binned him off during day one when he was unable to complete the Combat Fitness Test – an eight-mile run with a bergen weighing 30lb. After Callam's ejection, Phil's head dropped. In the Prayers Meeting that night, I was on the fence with him, and was considering ejecting him, when Colin delivered a view from an alternative angle.

'I'll play devil's advocate with no. 07', he said. 'On all the tests he's been through, he comes up short in a lot of them. I'll put this to you, though: of all the ones who are up there on that wall, if you're pinned down by fire, who's the one who's coming to get you? He'd come right through a hail of bullets for you. It puts a different spin on it . . .'

This was an angle none of us had taken into account at the time. For a while it almost caused me to reconsider my opinion. Hoban had aggression for sure, he had loyalty, and he was certainly brave. If I were to tell him to do something in battle, he would have gone through with it, no question. All of these were great qualities for a solider in the Green Army. However, running through a hail of bullets isn't enough in the Special Forces. I wouldn't want to be on an extraction mission and have somebody lose his head, running at the enemy in a rage, guns blazing. He'd only end up being a casualty and a problem for the rest of us. The Special Forces are about being the Thinking Soldier. I needed people who were going to use their brains first, their balls second. Hoban lasted one more day, maybe two.

Prayers Meetings aren't just used for individual assessments, but for tactical planning, too, and during *SAS: Who Dares Wins*, Season One, the DS would decide how best to challenge our group the following day. One trick we used was to play the weakest against the strongest; to mentally challenge the recruits who might be experiencing doubts regarding their ability, which, I guarantee you, was every one of them at one point or another. If the body is struggling, a strong mind can haul it through. But flip it the other way and the results can be disastrous.

To sow those seeds of doubt, the DS would gather all the recruits together after every trial had finished on the course. They would then ask them individually to pick out somebody they considered to be the weakest member of the group. It was a simple test of character. If an individual was described by their peers as being 'shit' or 'ineffective', we wanted to see their response. Would they tell themselves, 'I might not have been the quickest up the hills, but I know for a fact that I don't have to be the strongest or even the smartest. I have to be a combination of everything'? Or would negativity eat away at them?

It also gave people a chance to learn about themselves. A good recruit says, 'OK, my peer doesn't rate me, but how am I to learn from it? How can I use that and flip it into a positive?' It teaches people how to handle a negative situation in Selection, especially if, deep down, they know they're running as fast as they're able and they're trying as hard as they can. That's when they're able to walk away from criticism with their heads held high. It's interesting: I reckon 95 per cent of people fail Selection, but I guarantee most of them will have dropped out thinking, 'I thought I was a good soldier, but that's not for me.' They've done it, though. They've given it their best shot, and they're better soldiers for it as a result.

Finding that 5 per cent – *those that can* – is a challenge in itself. And to discover that special mindset within an individual, to separate the good candidates from the bad, the DS have to analyse each and every person from all angles. The only way to do that is to use all the resources available.

That's when the Prayers Meeting comes in.

THE INTEL

COLIN: The routine transfers very well to the civilian world because the Prayers Meeting during Selection is just that: *a meeting*. It doesn't have to be a 360-degree examination of a group of individuals. (Though you could use it for that reason if you wanted.) Instead, it should be tailored to your particular requirements; a lot of organisations would benefit from a gathering of this kind, whether they take place once a week, once a month, or after a project has been concluded. These discussions could focus on:

- The execution of a completed contract
- Status reports on a project
- The relationship with a business partner
- The happiness of everyone within a team working towards a common goal
- The work of new members within a team or group

It's vital we spend time at the back end of a mission in order to learn and reflect, before feeding that information and experience into a future cycle. Still, you'd be surprised at how many people fail to do so. Often they suffer as a consequence, and I know from personal experience what happens when a group doesn't debrief properly.

In one job I had, everybody had been placed into teams, but there was very little communication between any of them. They were all data processing, though none of them were sharing that information across the company. Meanwhile, everybody was working so hard individually that they had no time to chat or interact properly. The workforce had become locked into an unpleasant cycle, and it was costing the company a lot financially.

Here's why.

Each person was given a workload. The guys getting the best results were financially rewarded, which quickly created competition between individuals and their respective teams. The result of this rewards system was a very unhealthy environment in which nobody wanted to communicate. Staff members were afraid of their 'rivals', or colleagues, beating them to bonuses. They had become insular and secretive.

But not me.

Because of my role, I was able to float between groups. One day, I noticed something odd: the prices being recorded for certain things were always constant, even though in real terms the daily prices would be fluctuating.

When I asked why that was happening, nobody had a clue.

'Hasn't anybody tried to find out why?' I asked.

Everybody shrugged.

'No one's got time to speak to us,' said one bloke. That's when I decided to make myself busy. I called head office and spoke to a team leader.

'Excuse me, I've got your sales tickets here,' I said. 'I've noticed that for the last week, you've sent these tickets up with the same pricing every single day. Why's that?'

The answer was pretty uninspiring.

'Well, yeah, they're up one day and down the next day. You know, it just takes too much time to alter the prices on a daily basis . . .'

Undeterred, I decided to do some more digging, and for the next month I made spread sheets – and, believe me, I'm not one for spread sheets. I worked out how much they would have saved had they fluctuated their pricing. It turned out to be a lot, even in a week, which worked out to be very significant if you applied that to a year, or a decade, across the entire company.

Now I don't have a maths degree. I'm not interested in numbers. In fact, I'd already decided that this job bored me. But it showed me one thing: a lack of communication can be costly. In business terms, I was a grunt. But I had walked into that company as an outsider with nothing to lose, and I'd been able to look at their working processes from a different angle because I wasn't locked into a culture of insular thinking. That had helped me to spot a massive oversight.

My discovery shook things up a little. The firm subsequently established its equivalent of the Prayers Meeting comprising a group of team leaders. They could see their working practices from different angles for the first time and it altered their way of thinking. The wastage was acknowledged and established, and the pricing system was altered accordingly, creating a huge upturn.

All that from one shrewd person making himself useful.

Now see your team, your situation, your issues, and imagine what a regular Prayers Meeting might do for *you*.

PART THREE
CONFLICT

INTRODUCTION

Rhythmically, everyday life can be like war. That might seem dramatic, but it's true. People get into a dispute; arguments and disagreements can take place almost anywhere. There are underlying politics and social tension in most offices and teams, and we often fail to see the flashpoints coming. An angry clash can kick off when we least expect it, leaving us stressed and destabilised. But conflict is what the Special Forces deal in, and we're adept at handling it.

While the violent episodes we experience in the SAS (hopefully) won't play a part in your life, the techniques and tactics we employ to manage conflict, such as calming flashpoints, can be put to very good use in a civilian context. In this next section, we'll detail how to stay calm and focused in the heat of battle, the techniques needed to maximise victory and learn from defeat, and the psychological mindset required to execute an unpleasant task when working towards the greater good.

COLIN: After I'd joined the Army, I studied Conflict Resolution at university. That education, combined with my military experience, means I've often been asked to present talks on the subject at colleges and in large companies. Whenever I start a lecture, I always ask the group to think of an alternative word for the term 'conflict' and the answers are always the same:

'War.'

'Fighting.'

'Battle.'

Those responses are wide of the mark, however, which, in itself, is one of the problems with conflict: the above words are all a consequence of it; they're what take place as a result of conflict, and often they have very little to do with the original point of the dispute. Rather, they're ugly afterthoughts.

Conflict should be viewed as the point of disagreement between two or more parties. In a military sense, this usually involves a political dispute between nations. Or, in other words, *war, fighting, battles.* They're the results of a squabble between opposing parties, and the most logical decision to make once conflict begins is to establish the common goal between those two opposing forces. Once that has taken place, it's far easier to reach a point of resolution. Sadly, what usually occurs is the destructive consequences of conflict.

How the British Army deals with the fallout from political disputes was my job for a long while and I've seen the ugly results at close hand. When I served with the Royal Scots, I was posted in Northern Ireland during the Troubles, and while it wasn't a war as such, it could still be bloody and brutal.

People were shot in front of me, including one colleague who was killed by the infamous 'Armagh Sniper', a member of the IRA who eventually murdered nine British soldiers between 1990 and 1997.

While that period in my life was fairly stressful, it wasn't until I had joined the SAS and worked in Sierra Leone and the Gulf War that I got a real sense of the awful intensity of conflict. In Northern Ireland, we would go out for four hour-long patrols where we had to be switched on at the highest level for several hours. But in Iraq our guard was up 24/7, unless we were sleeping, and even then it was hard to relax because we'd come to expect an attack at almost any moment. Mental stress was constantly burning away at me, and the only way to get around it was to try to switch off by watching films or sport on the TV, anything that would take me away from the horrors of war for a while. Hitting the gym helped to keep my head steady as well. Clear thinking was vital.

A sense of balance is vital in civilian life, too. When we're entangled in the consequences of conflict, the situations we find ourselves in are usually destructive, both to the people directly involved and those around us. Our actions can become irrational. We can panic and make drastic decisions when shrewd-thinking is called for. The results might be negative and long lasting, and there is usually collateral damage. But how we operate within conflict situations is often the sole determining factor in reaching a successful conclusion.

We can be involved in a dispute at home which affects everyone in the household; a clash between two colleagues on the same team can result in diminished productivity and damaged team morale. Saying the wrong thing to our boss or client in the heat of a dispute might result in us being sacked or losing business. Financially, that could prove disastrous.

But flashpoints can be avoided and resolved; peaceful resolution is always within our reach, especially when the collateral damage in civilian life is often social or financial. Nobody is going to die because of a boardroom dispute or an argument over a parking space in the supermarket. But that doesn't mean those situations aren't in need of some seriously quick-thinking. In the Special Forces we have battle-tested psychological mechanisms that allow us to think clearly when the gunfire raging around us is aggressive and intense. We know when to retreat and how to learn from defeat. It's instilled in us that we should maximise every victory. There is also the issue of dirty work and how performing an ugly task (one that might have a negative impact on ourselves or the people around us) can be the wisest decision in order to achieve long-term success. Our training has taught us to seek out the path of least resistance when seeking resolution in any situation. Now it can help you, too.

THE BALANCE OF AGGRESSION

ANT: A lot of people think that gunfights and conflict are about aggression and bravery. They believe the Special Forces rely solely on brute force to get the job done. That might be the case in some elements of the military, but it's not a way of thinking that has a home in an organisation such as the SBS, where the ideal operation is a swift job that passes quietly, without a round being fired. Sadly, that happens very rarely. When missions go noisy, aggression comes into play, but it's always controlled. We don't run around like headless chickens, shooting blindly at the enemy. Instead we use our anger like any other resource: if ever it's required, we are able to turn it on and off like a tap.

I've found that people often show reckless aggression when they lose control, or find themselves in a situation that places them outside their comfort zone. They lash out in an attempt to escape, either verbally, tactically or physically. Often, they end up attacking wildly. They run towards their own death because they haven't paused to think. They've failed to establish a new plan and as a result they make terrible mistakes in the heat of the moment.

I know because I've been there myself, though it's only ever happened to me in civilian life. I've been in situations where someone has taken the piss or attacked me and I've become involved in a row. My subconscious flicked the aggression on and I flew into a rage. The next thing I knew, I'd smacked someone, and it's not been pretty.

I'm not proud of it.

Age and maturity have since taken that out of me, as has my training. I've learned to walk away from situations where my aggression might once have got me into trouble because I know that when that switch is flicked, I find it difficult to locate the off button.

During missions I've always been able to control my aggression quite easily, probably because my life was often at stake. I couldn't be reckless: a thoughtless act might have killed me or one of my pals. Keeping my head together on a mission was vital. A whole team were depending on me to remain calm under pressure; operations were reliant on the team acting effectively. Our overall objective was always a good focus for me and I kept the goal in mind at all times. The threat of dying helped, too.

I've also used aggression to help me through moments of pain. During the Hills Phase on Selection, we would run across the Brecon Beacons every day. One of the marches seemed to go on forever and everybody hits the pain barrier four or five times before they finish. At one point, I thought, 'I can't go on any more. I'm done . . .'

That's when I flicked the switch. Aggression drove me on. It ordered me to quit complaining and get angry. That emotion pushed me past the pain and got me through; I was able to grit my teeth and summon an extra reserve of energy. It gave me a new lease of life and ensured I passed through to the next stage of Selection.

COLIN: Because of my military experience, I have a different perspective on flashpoint incidents. I see people become enraged while driving and it doesn't faze me. I don't get stressed when someone challenges me in an aggressive manner during a meeting. As a result of some of the things I've seen during combat, I'm able to think, 'In the grand scheme of things, this situation doesn't really matter.' That doesn't mean those situations are lacking in intensity, however. Flashpoint moments and conflict can be incredibly stressful if we're not used to facing up to the challenge involved. But applying the techniques learned by the *SAS: Who Dares Wins* team will keep you calm in the most stressful or volatile situations. Battle scenarios will become manageable, *malleable*. Your decision-making under stress will feel measured.

Ultimately, it could be the difference between success and failure.

12

MOVING INTO IMMEDIATE ACTION (WHAT TO DO WHEN THINGS GO BADLY WRONG)

We all experience moments when life blows up in our faces. It could be that a DIY project at home has fallen apart at the seams or a contractor has let you down. Maybe a pub dispute with a friend has blown up and is threatening to develop into a fight. Or perhaps you've been aggressively challenged about your capabilities when performing a particular task or role at work.

In the SAS vernacular, your situation has 'gone noisy'. It's so called because in most cases a stressful problem involves a gunfight, which can be very testing on the eardrums. And like most violent shit shows, any conflict scenario, such as the ones mentioned above, can rapidly get out of hand without a period of clear thinking. Moving into cover, or buying yourself some breathing space while planning your next move, is vital. Doing it is a lot easier than you might think, too . . .

COLIN: In real life, bullets make a funny noise when they're fired at you. It's not a series of explosions – *BANG! BANG! BANG!* – the kind you might hear in a Hollywood blockbuster. Instead, they arrive in a series of short, sharp whistles as they whip past – *Ptzzzt! Ptzzzt! Ptzzzt!* After that, those little lead wasps usually hit a nearby wall or other surface with a loud pop. (Unless you've been hit, of course, and then, there's no sound at all.) The moment that first round flashes past is usually the moment that our training kicks in, and life seems to go into slow motion.

If one thing's certain in the SAS, it's that missions rarely go to plan and bullets are often the first indication that an operation has changed course entirely. It's time to rethink our course of action. That's not normally a problem, though – even if one of our colleagues has been hit or the squadron has been pinned down by enemy fire – because we always prepare for the worst-case scenario during the Planning and Briefing

Phases by working out our Immediate Action, or IA – a fallback plan that we're able to rely on in order to get out of trouble.

In layman's terms, we have two types of Plan B – the long-term plan, or Direct Action (DA), and the short-term one, which is called Immediate Action (IA). Direct Action is the easier to deal with because it's something that we would have anticipated as a result of intelligence or our own experience. So, for example, when planning for a raid on a military compound, we might agree to retreat to a certain position should we find it impossible to breach a defensive wall. Once we've done so, an air attack can move in.

On other occasions, we'll opt to move out of an area, or country, altogether for extraction because we've been overrun and suffered heavy casualties in the process. In those cases, there are certain predetermined escape routes. Should we then miss our scheduled communications following a mission, our forces would know roughly the direction we would aim to head in, and could then pick us up if necessary.

The DA never changes. It's the unexpected, short-term IAs that can become the most disruptive, and they tend to happen on a daily basis. We can't prepare for them, either. But we can learn how to react when things start to go wrong.

LEARN TO REACT

OLLIE: I've found that training and experience are the best routes to handling short-term Immediate Actions, and in a warzone they can involve all kinds of scenarios. Maybe we've encountered stronger enemy resistance than expected, a rocket-launcher that comes out of nowhere or an IED field that wasn't picked up by the intelligence services. I've been unexpectedly pinned down by enemy contact too many times to count. There have been situations where my squadron was dominated by far superior numbers, with more firepower, but we still survived because we were able to construct an effective IA.

The most memorable occasion was when I was working as a security manager in Iraq. It's funny: I think I experienced more contact during my time as a civilian than I did in the Special Forces, which was hardly suprising given I spent so long in enemy territory, but my training kept me alive. On this occasion, my job was to protect the major media teams covering the occupation efforts, while helping to protect the rebuilding of Baghdad's infrastructure. At one point, I had 2,000 Iraqis working for me, guys we were training to be bodyguards, but, as you can imagine, that made us a target for the local militia groups. They claimed our Iraqi allies were being 'Westernised', and we were sometimes attacked, but regardless of what happened I never forgot my training. I had learned that being a Special Forces soldier meant operating in the heat of the moment, assessing a situation very quickly, and deciding upon the best IA. It saved my neck on more than one occasion.

Such an attack took place in a village just north of Baghdad. We were resting up in a compound, when the first wave of bullets came in. I felt them first, little whips of air fizzing past my head. Immediately, everybody hit the ground, and we took cover. When I looked up, I could see that a group of enemy soldiers had taken up positions behind our vehicles. There were others located in nearby buildings. Heavy fire was being laid down on us from all angles. Rounds ricocheted off the ground and nearby walls. We were easily outnumbered, and I could sense the situation getting out of control.

With bullets raining down, I had to formulate a short-term IA. The first thing to do was to evaluate our situation. The only exit route was an access point positioned towards the top of the compound: the other doors were covered by enemy forces. That's when I realised another escape path might open up if we were to trick our attackers. Shaping to move towards the exit on the left-hand side could encourage them to concentrate their fire on that one spot, allowing us to escape via another route. So I sent one of my men to move to our false exit route, telling him to pop up every now and then, thus giving the impression we were making our way over as a group.

Our attackers fell for it almost immediately. They changed formation in an attempt to dominate that position, and as soon as they moved, another path to our vehicles was freed up. We pegged it, jumping into the cars and driving off, rounds whistling through the windows as we exited. As we left them, I remember thinking, 'Where had that IA come from?' I couldn't even remember thinking it up at first. Our exit strategy had just *happened*. But that's what occurs when someone has been so highly trained, like myself. I had experienced pressurised contact situations before, so solutions to them came naturally. I just had to trust my gut.

With hindsight, nothing I could have done during the Planning or Briefing Phases of our Mission Success Cycle that day would have prepared us for that attack. It had been a complete surprise, but it was a valuable reminder for me. As in life, problems and issues can come out of nowhere, no matter how well we organise ourselves. In fact, the best way to prepare is to always expect that *something* might go wrong because it keeps us in an alert frame of mind, which is vital for coming up with the best IA possible.

READY YOURSELF FOR THE WORST

ANT: Don't kid yourself. You can't predict where or when a shit storm will hit, but you can ready yourself for it. When I first joined the Special Forces, I amplified certain personal attributes such as physical robustness and discipline, but I also worked on my attention to detail. That was often vital in the heat of the battle, because remembering minor pieces of information often saved lives.

Don't believe me? Well, just imagine for a second that we're in a warzone together. There are rounds going off, left, right and centre. Suddenly, you get shot in the leg – and it's bad. Relax. I can help you. I know where your medi kit's been stashed because I asked you a couple of days back – that's the level of attention to detail that's been drilled into us on Selection. Within seconds I'm going to grab your tourniquet, apply it to the wound, and stop you from bleeding out. I've probably saved your life before you've even had a chance to come round and scream for morphine. But if you're dead, also know that I'm going to acquire everything you've got – grenades, medical equipment and magazines – within seconds, just in case I need them later on.

Now, I'm not sure what kind of office you work in, but I'm guessing you won't be requiring any ammo or morphine during a deadline crisis. (Or maybe you do?) Still, you can function during a worst-case scenario, but only if you work on your attention to detail. So imagine your boss has gone down sick as an important project hits deadline day, with a vital presentation booked in with a client:

- Do you know where they kept the contract notes for that project?
- Where was the presentation due to take place and with whom?
- And who's your next best person for the presentation? *Because they're going instead.*

Attention to detail can give us the information we need in a crisis. It allows us to have all the facts at our disposal when formulating a Plan B. Without it, we might well be heading into a shit storm of our own.

THE INTEL

OLLIE: Everyone needs a preferred DA for any project they're undertaking, no matter what that might be. These are

Plan Bs. The DA is one we can prepare for in advance; the IA hits us out of the blue. How we think on our DAs is usually dependent on the issues we think might challenge us during the Delivery Phase. For a clearer idea of what those hurdles might be, we should always refer to the threats that were first established during the Planning Phase of the Mission Success Cycle. From there we can work out what strategies to use should those problems then arise. Some examples of these could include:

- A key member of staff is going on holiday at a busy time in the project. How do we fill the gaps?
- Payments owed to us might come in late next month. Can we navigate the shortfall with a loan?
- A self-employed person has to figure out their tax returns next week. How will they make up for the working days lost to accountancy tasks?
- Our company is implementing a new computer software system. Is somebody from the IT department briefed to react to any failures that might occur at key stages during a project?

With long-term DAs in place, issues such as the above become much easier to resolve. However, nobody can really prepare a short-term IA, a response to those unforeseen nightmares that sucker-punch us from out of nowhere. In those situations, we need to rely on experience and instinct as best we can. Sadly, what tends to happen to anyone when they've been shocked by an unexpected issue is that they let their negative feelings and emotions take over. They mope or panic. They dally. And before they know it, a bad situation has become ten times worse. In the Special Forces we're trained to implement our IA decisively and positively, with the following five steps.

1. React as quickly as possible. Run an evaluation of the situation. What's the best way of getting out of it? Then ask yourself the question: Is right now the opportune moment to execute my IA? Or will breathing space reduce the threat of putting myself in further jeopardy with a hasty decision?

2. Draw on training and experience. They're what allow us to rely on our gut instincts; with them we can react effectively and with confidence. Why? Because our reactions would have been created from knowledge we have previously gained – from a training course or a similar situation, for example. Education and intel should encourage us to act on initiative.

    A great example of this thought process was evident when, in 2015, a gunman emerged from the toilet of a moving Parisian train with an AK-47 slung over his shoulder. He was preparing to commit a terrorist attack. There would have been no escape for anyone onboard because the train was moving at high speed and it was impossible to get off. Luckily, a holidaying US airman had noticed him acting suspiciously moments earlier. When he heard him loading his weapon in the toilet, the airman decided to fight. With the help of two other travelling companions (one of whom was also in the US military), he jumped the terrorist, saving hundreds of lives in what would have been a massacre.

Afterwards a lot of people asked, 'How did those guys know to jump him? Why didn't they freeze?' Well, it was because two of them had training. A lot of people see a gun and they understandably become paralysed with fear. That off-duty military officer was different: he understood how long it took to squeeze off a round; he was familiar with the process of reloading a magazine; he would have been able to spot the smaller details, such as whether the gun's safety catch was on or off.

Because of his training and experience, that information would have been quickly processed, in the same way that surgeons' training enables them to understand when a patient might be approaching critical condition, or computer code programmers can tell when their software is being hacked. Knowledge and experience are our greatest weapons in times of trouble.

3. In any situation we generally have three options: fight, flight or freeze. We should never do the latter. Procrastination breeds over-thinking, and closes our window of opportunity. Get aggressive, or retreat, but never stop.

Short-term IAs are instinctive. Like the passengers on that Parisian train, we have to trust our gut feelings. If we start thinking too much about a situation that requires swift resolution, that's when we screw up. We over-complicate things mentally and physically. In a military sense that's very dangerous because it can place us in a deteriorating situation, one we might not be able to escape from.

4. As Ant explained earlier, attention to detail is key. It might rescue a team effort or project when a problem is apparently becoming uncontrollable.

5. Find the line of least resistance in any situation. This is a tactic that works well in both civilian and military situations. How can you escape quickly with the minimum amount of conflict, arguments or disputes? Any idiot can stand there and fight to the death, but that's not the Thinking Soldier's way. It's not the tactic employed by the greatest business minds and leaders, either. If we're in trouble, let's not make things harder for ourselves.

It's very easy to become involved in a dispute with a work colleague or client during the execution of a project. If conflict is occurring over a minor detail, it's often the smarter play to accept that both parties are unlikely to reach an agreement in a short space of time. In those cases we should move on with the primary objective. If we allow ourselves to become bogged down over a small element, the whole mission can be endangered. Instead, look for the escape route that offers the fewest possible bumps in the road.

13

BREATHE.
RECALIBRATE.
DELIVER.
(HOW TO STAY CALM
UNDER PRESSURE)

Keeping calm under intense stress isn't easy, especially when it feels as if one wrong move could heighten tensions or cause a situation to escalate very quickly. But with the help of our easy-to-use psychological playbook, you'll soon be able to maintain a level of calm and make decisions quickly and effectively, while everybody around you panics . . .

OLLIE: 'No plan survives first contact.'

That's what tends to happen in our line of work: things go wrong, people start shooting. The real skill in the Special Forces is being able to operate effectively under the intense stress of a situation that is constantly changing and to perform our IAs without freaking out.

It's the same for you as well. Whatever the problem that's landed in your lap, it's important to maintain calm and function normally if things start going unexpectedly wrong. The big question is, *how*?

Well, for the most part, the Special Forces use a simple mantra that keeps us level-headed under extreme pressure:

Breathe.

Recalibrate.

Deliver.

It might not sound like much, but it's a surefire way of regaining control in any situation that might be heading in a dangerous direction, and it's definitely saved my life on more than one occasion. Let me walk you through it.

1. BREATHE

Whenever any scenario goes haywire, Special Forces soldiers will first revisit their training – and in a heartbeat. We've been taught that the brain can only process between five and nine pieces of information at a time – any more than that and it becomes confused; it reacts in a way that's disruptive.

In military terms, a soldier might have travelled hundreds

of miles by air, sea and land to get to their objective. They're tired and they're hungry. Suddenly something goes wrong. Within seconds there are seven, eight, nine things to think about – *enemy contact, injured soldier, escape routes, fatigue, dangerous extraction location, possible IEDs, escaping target, air support* – but their body doesn't want to function; it's going into defence mode, and it wants to close down. It has reached *breakpoint.*

That term is key here. The definition of breakpoint is 'an intentional stopping or pausing place in a computer program, put in for debugging purposes'. In the Special Forces we've been trained to understand when our personal breakpoint is approaching, and from there we can 'debug' ourselves. It could begin when bullets start raining down or if we've been captured. That's when we breathe – twice, deeply – and pause for a couple of seconds. It prevents us from making rash decisions and helps us to regain control of a pressurised situation. From there we can debug and react effectively – we find a second or two to think.

In the civilian world, the issues are just as complex. For example, an individual might face a crisis at work, but there's a range of other challenges to be faced: picking the kids up from school or taking the dog to the vet's, the car needs to be fixed, then there's a nasty bill still to be paid; people are coming round for dinner and there's shopping to be done; *'Where's the mobile?'* It's easy for people to wilt under the pressure and blow up at someone. But breathing and debugging can often be the difference between being able to defuse a situation and doing something rash, when you think later, 'I wish I hadn't done that . . .'

I've used this debug method effectively many times. One occasion was in Iraq when I was again working as a private security contractor, shortly after leaving the Special Forces. I had been guarding a company that was travelling in a convoy of five cars towards Baghdad, shortly after the fall of Saddam Hussein. His regime had blown up; life was lawless. The team had plenty of cash and lots of expensive equipment, which was why they needed my team to shepherd them safely through Jordan and Iraq. I was driving the rear car; my body armour was in place, an MP5 Kurz rested on my lap.

Behind me was a colleague, who was armed with an AK-47. Then, out of nowhere on a deserted road, I saw flashing lights behind us. A car was zooming into view in my wing mirror and once it came close, machine guns poked out of every window. I could see Arab headdresses behind as bullets started *pop-pop-popping* above our heads. We were 12 hours into the journey and I was exhausted. Suddenly, I felt my five-to-nine capacity filling up, which was when I ducked down into my seat and sucked in two deep, settling breaths to calm myself down . . .

2. RECALIBRATE

. . . Then I debugged; *I recalibrated.*

I quickly established what was happening. My guess

was that our attackers had been tipped off by the checkpoint guards we had passed an hour or so previously. The cars had been searched as we entered the country from Jordan and the value of our equipment wouldn't have gone unnoticed. A phone call must have been made to militias at Ramadi and Fallujah and now their plan was to force us off the road, presumably to pillage and execute us.

OK, so that was the situation. *But how the hell were we supposed to get out of it?* At first I thought about flooring the car and legging it to Baghdad as fast as we could, but I worried our attackers would shoot out the convoy. The tyres would be targeted first of all. Then, once all the vehicles had been disabled, it was highly likely we would be surrounded, dragged from the cars and shot on the side of the road. With my brain now recalibrated, I realised we had only one option if we were to survive. *get aggressive.*

3. DELIVER

It was time to put ideas into action.

Tactically, I knew the militia's first move would be to shoot out our leading car because that would force us all to slow down. With that in mind, I pulled into the road's central lane, which invited them to accelerate ahead of us. But it was also a trap: with our vehicles now in line and another car ahead, they were boxed in. Meanwhile, our windows were up, so nobody had spotted my colleague and myself lifting our weapons. Once I'd given the order to fire, we rained bullets on the gunmen. Shells and glass exploded everywhere. We didn't stop firing until their car had rolled to a halt on the roadside, smoke pumping from the engine.

Breathe.

Recalibrate.

Deliver.

That one mantra had saved my life. Without it, I could have panicked and lost control. Instead, I was able to slow the situation down in my mind and decide upon the best course of action, before seeing it through.

THE INTEL

So, what can *you* take from my experience? It's simple really. When your life gets noisy, when you feel overwhelmed by factors that seem out of control, or if a situation, or person, is unexpectedly dictating your actions, remember the mantra: *Breathe. Recalibrate. Deliver.*

- Breathe. *Say a surprisingly huge bill has dropped through the letterbox, or a massive cock-up has taken place at work (one that's your fault): don't freak out. Breathe twice – deeply.*
- Recalibrate – debug. Consider your options. *Can you borrow some money in the short term? What's the best way of atoning for your error or correcting the situation? Establish your most effective course of action in that moment.*

- Deliver. Settle on a plan, then carry it out to the best of your ability.

Your crisis moment could happen in work, at home or in the street. But using those three words should prevent you from making any rash decisions that might carry regrettable consequences further down the line.

14

HOW TO CONTROL YOUR EMOTIONS

It's easy to become over-emotional in life, especially when the pressure is rising. We get passionate about work and hate to see our ideas fail. At home, small frustrations can build up during the day and a minor, unrelated incident might cause us to explode, upsetting our loved ones, and causing somebody to say something that they might regret later.

In the Special Forces, there's very little room for feelings. We don't dwell on death or allow quests for revenge to diminish our focus. Successes are dealt with functionally and there is never any celebration when capturing a high-profile target or nailing a seemingly

© Anthony Middleton

Anthony 'Ant' Middleton in Afghanistan during his time in the Service.

© Ryan McNamara

Ant on location on SAS 1

© Jason Fox

Jason 'Foxy' Fox in Afghanistan

© Ryan McNamara

Foxy on location on SAS 1

Matthew 'Ollie' Ollerton in Iraq, just after the fall of Saddam Hussein

Ollie on location on SAS 1

Colin Maclachlan in 2000

Colin in the interrogation room of the SAS 1 set

Anthony Middleton instructs Phil Hoban in map reading on Day 1 of SAS filming

Recruits learn vital navigation skills on Day 1 of SAS filming

Foxy and Ollie use their downtime for a workout in the 'pain cave'

Ollie leads contributors Caine, Alan and Ryan on the
CFT (combat fitness test) on Day 1 of SAS 1 filming

Recruits take a break after the CFT on Day 1 of SAS 1 filming

Recruit line-up on Day 1 of SAS 1 filming

impossible mission. The reason for this is clear: stripping
away emotions allows us to perform more effectively; we get
the job done better. Carrying that attitude into civilian life will
quickly reap rewards.

COLIN: Emotions can cloud our judgement, but only

if we allow them to. Fear, sadness, joy, anxiety and jealousy:
these are just some of the factors that alter how we function
in a variety of circumstances. Anger can change the way we
make a business decision, likewise the fear of failure. Meanwhile, we might react to a person in a certain way because we
feel guilty or embarrassed about something that has previously
taken place between us. Happiness could cause us to lower
our guard when we need to be at our most cautious.

The important thing to remember about emotion is that
we are the gatekeepers of our thoughts, nobody else. Sure,
somebody might hope to terrify us, or they might want to create
a sense of shame, but that doesn't mean they'll necessarily
succeed. In fact, they're only able to achieve those aims if we
allow them to. Understanding that reality is a very powerful first
step towards gaining a handle on how to remain emotionally
stable during difficult situations.

In the Special Forces, emotions are often amplified
because we regularly operate in such challenging conditions,
but civilian life brings its own stresses, too. Pressure comes
with exams, driving tests, legal issues, business deals, deadlines, health problems, financial concerns and family worries;
it can be caused by an expectation of success or the awful

consequences of failure, and poor emotional control can lead to poor decision-making.

Take professional sport as an example. The tennis star Andy Murray has too often allowed emotion to dictate his performance levels, especially at the beginning of his career, when he would blow up at the slightest mistake. It wasn't uncommon to see him lose his serve and then explode in a rage. Within no time at all, he would be a set down because he had lost emotional stability. But failure can also happen at the opposite end of the scale. How often have we criticised a team for not showing enough passion and commitment during an important fixture?

When it comes to controlling our feelings, the Special Forces are expected to maintain balance during operations, and to do so we constantly remind ourselves of the task in hand. Why? Because it helps to remove any emotion from our decision-making process. After all, it's our job to focus on the bigger prize rather than sweating the smaller issues. So, during a high-threat detention operation, we direct all our efforts towards finding the target rather than any peripheral issues that might emotionally unbalance us, such as the threat of capture (fear), a dead teammate (grief) or poor intel (anger, frustration). Rushing into a hail of bullets because we're angry, and dragging everyone else along with us, isn't going to do anybody any good.

To ensure that our mission focus is maintained, a team leader will always state an objective *twice* during briefings. So, for example, 'Our mission is to detain the target. *Our mission is to detain the target.'* Every time the mission is mentioned in that first briefing, the objective is repeated. 'Our mission is to detain the target. *Our mission is to detain the target.'* That technique embeds the primary objective into everybody's mind, so if the shit starts hitting the fan, we've been reminded that our position isn't to shoot all the enemy attacking us in a rage or to evade imprisonment out of fear. Instead our mission is to detain the target. (*Our mission is to detain the target.*)

Introducing that one technique into team meetings or briefings, would help a lot of businesses to sharpen their focus. It can also help us as individuals, especially people who might operate on a shorter fuse or suffer from anxiety problems. Having a bigger picture in mind often distracts us from any emotional flaws we might have.

I've often put this theory into practice. I was once captured and tortured by enemy soldiers. I had been operating on a secret mission with another agent when our car broke down. From there, we had two options: wait for a military convoy to collect us or hijack a taxi. We went for the latter, flagging down a cab and bundling the driver into the back seat at gunpoint, but when we got to a checkpoint just outside the city, there were about 20 enemy soldiers waiting for us. And when a car came around the front to block us off, another parking at our rear, I knew we were in trouble. We had been fronted and tailed. The soldiers then started waving machine guns around. Several warning shots were fired from both sides, and as we emerged from the car, I was smashed around the back of the head by the butt of an AK-47. The blow dazed me and before long I was in a dark room. I'd been handcuffed to a railing.

The first beating was awful. As they tore at my clothes, I fought back with punches and head butts. Amid all the pain and the stress, I made a mental deal with myself: 'I'm not going to give up easily here,' I thought. 'For every blow to the head with a rifle butt, I'll drop an item of clothing – only one though.' It became a game to distract myself from the fear that could quite easily have overwhelmed me.

That's when the first mock execution took place. I was shoved against a wall and the muzzle of an AK-47 was pressed into the back of my skull. My captors were shouting in Arabic. I had learned the language and could tell they were keen to finish me off, there and then. There was even talk of getting a video camera to film my death for a propaganda film.

'I'm done,' I thought.

And that's when emotion kicked in for the first time. Strangely, there wasn't any fear. I hadn't been worried about dying. Instead there was a flicker of sadness at how my parents would react to the news of my death. If the details of my capture and beatings made it back to them, it would have been impossible for them to cope with the news. That brought up a rush of emotion. I knew it might cause me to act irrationally, so to regain control I returned my focus to the mission in hand. Even though part of our mission had been completed we were only halfway through our task at that point. We had to return to base camp. *We had to return to base camp.* Worrying about my parents and their grief wasn't going to save either of us.

The fact that my colleague was in a cell next to me also helped to sharpen my resolve – I had to get him back with me, and I understood that our best chance of survival hinged on us both remaining calm. Anger, fear and worry would have to wait, because we would have only limited chances to complete our mission; we had to remain alert to every possible opportunity, whether that be a break-out or the tactical decision to stay put; a chance to alert the British forces might present itself; one of us might even discover a way of leaving signals, clues as to where we were being held. But our endgame was always the same. *We had to return to base camp.*

There were six mock executions in total, each one more horrific than the last, until eventually we were bundled into a car and driven to another enemy stronghold. I noted every junction and landmark we passed along the way. I didn't know whether that information might come in handy at some point, but my training had taught me to make the most of every source of intel available to me. It also helped me to think straight as I tried to figure out where the hell we were going. Luckily for us, those landmarks didn't come into play. Intel alerted base that we had been captured and a rescue mission took place.

All I could hear as my Special Forces colleagues bundled me into the back of a Range Rover was the sound of rocket-propelled grenades being fired behind us. You might have thought that emotion would have taken over at that point – that happiness and relief would flood over me – but it didn't. I couldn't allow it to. Instead, I remained alert to the importance of our overall objective and what had just taken place. I realised that we had lost vital pieces of kit during our capture, although we understood collateral damage as being a regrettable part of the job.

Instead, during that moment of relative security, I thought of one thing only: I was returning to base, where my mission would be completed. *I had to return to base camp.*

THE INTEL

- Before every mission, repeat your objective twice. It will help you to remain focused, particularly in a situation where emotion might come into play. *So, let's imagine we're approaching a work appraisal. It's taking place with a management figure we've clashed with in the past; the pair of us haven't seen eye to eye. In the build-up to the conversation, think of the objective – 'I want to get a pay rise', or 'I want to take on more responsibility.' Say it twice. Imprint it on your brain. If the meeting begins to take a turn for the worse, use it to prevent emotion creeping in.*

- In any high-pressure situation, emotion can destabilise us, especially those of us who might have short fuses or anxiety issues. So first regain composure with two deep, settling breaths. Remember, we are the gatekeepers of our emotions. Regain control.

- Recalibrate #1. Recognise the emotion that's taking hold; understand why it's there. Then think about how it might take you off course. Will fear cause you to run? Is anger going to affect your control? Is sadness going to cause you to quit?

- Recalibrate #2. Remind yourself of the mission objective. Then remind yourself again. A renewed focus should suppress the feelings affecting your judgement.
- Now deliver.

15
HOW TO AVOID CONFLICT

Spotting a brewing conflict can be a godsend. It allows us to resolve any trouble before an ugly situation becomes unmanageable. Often the signs are there for all of us to see, but how we respond to them is key, and the right plays can help us to head off trouble.

Quick thinking is vital in a warzone, where firing a round is often considered to be a last resort. It's just as important in any civilian environment where people regularly come into contact and conflict with one another: anger and aggression should usually be avoided at all costs. In the Special Forces we used a number of techniques to avoid those unnecessary, and always ugly, flashpoints. Some of them might help you to avoid a battle of your own.

COLIN: It's always wise to avoid conflict if you can. I should know. I've been on many a patrol in Iraq and witnessed how one ill-advised gesture can lead to reprisals from an angry mob. Those incidents quickly taught me that smart thinking and diplomacy were the most effective ways of halting conflict. Intelligence allows us to see trouble coming and most cases communication, not aggression, is the most effective tool we have at our disposal.

While operating in Baghdad during the second Gulf War, I was attached to a new unit and what I noticed immediately was that they had a very different mindset to the people I'd been working with previously. My former colleagues were more laid-back: during patrols in Basra we would cut about without helmets, our weapons were usually held down by our sides and we would never take heavy armour out with us. But these guys were different. They moved in armoured vehicles and their posture was very aggressive. Whenever a car approached they would aim their weapons at the windscreens.

I would head out with them every day, and on one patrol we turned the corner and there was a big mob waiting for us. The Commanding Officer shouted out his orders.

'Bring the M16 machine gun up,' he said. 'Get the barrel on, and bring the armoured car to the front of the crowd.'

But I had a different plan. I knew a calmer approach, and the subtleties of body language, would give us a better chance of working through the crowd without incident.

'Wait, give me two minutes,' I said. 'Let me take the dog handler . . .'

A large Alsatian dog, with its handler, was often attached to a Special Forces unit. Dogs were particularly handy when looking for drugs or guns and, interestingly, they were also a bit of a novelty in that part of the world, and rather intimidating. That made them a useful tool when attempting to stop a crowd in its tracks without being too aggressive. I took off my helmet and kept my firearm at my side. With the dog handler and his animal walking six feet behind me, I approached a man who introduced himself as the leader. Because I was able to speak some Arabic, we were able to chat fairly easily. He explained how worried the people in that area had become. Their road networks had been blown to bits so travelling around was fraught with danger. Sometimes, when an Iraqi car went within 100 metres of a military vehicle, usually accidentally, they were shot at.

I nodded. 'Yeah, I get that,' I said sympathetically. 'It's a new country for the military forces here and they're creating rules to protect themselves.'

I called over the major who was travelling with us and introduced him to the tribal elder.

'You need to respect this guy,' I told him. 'He basically runs this community.'

They got talking. Before long, information was being shared. The Iraqi leader was able to point the forces in the direction of some local workers who would be ideal for a bridge-building project that had to take place in the wake of the invasion. With the diplomatic approach, I was able to prevent a worrying situation from turning nasty. Smart thinking and diplomacy, not aggression, had resolved a potential conflict, and I've since found that this approach is easily transferable to the civilian world.

Every time two groups go head to head with opposing thoughts, emotions or ideas, there is the potential for conflict, and that applies to politics, the workplace, at home – or even out on the street. At that flashpoint in Baghdad, two opposing forces came together like two gangs of rival football fans. When that happens, any aggressive posturing can explode into violence. When two office rivals become entangled in dispute, communication can get messy. The key is to diffuse the danger before it gets out of hand, but how?

CONTROL YOUR EMOTIONS

I had chosen to take the proactive but conciliatory approach. I knew by moving towards the group in a civil manner, rather than pointing my weapon, I had more chance of keeping a lid on any rising tension. The first rule of conflict avoidance is to remain calm: in a dispute, if we get emotional and shout, we lose; if we lash out, we relinquish control. And that's not just applicable to the theatre of combat. It's relevant to any form of dispute. How many times have we blown up in a work dispute only to regret it afterwards?

As mentioned previously, it's important to remember that only we can manage our emotions in any conflict – nobody else. We can choose whether to shout or stay calm. And the latter is always preferable: it allows us to retain control and maintain a better perspective on any given situation.

APPROACH EVERY SITUATION WITH A PEACEFUL CONCLUSION IN MIND

Whenever Special Forces go on a mission, our language generally focuses on words and phrases associated with a peaceful resolution. If we were moving in on a hostage rescue operation, our instructions would be to 'save the hostages'. Never would anyone tell us to 'kill as many of the enemy as possible'. Sometimes there are occasions where we have to shoot somebody, especially when we're operating on a high-threat detention mission. Overall, though, the perfect operation is one where we move in and out without the alarm being raised.

In Baghdad it helped that I was able to find a common objective with the tribal elder. I expressed our willingness to build a bridge that would help both the Western military and the local people. With that common goal in mind, it made sense that we could find a way to work together. It might be that, within a civilian setting, two separate teams in a company join forces to improve their working practices. Or, as another example, think of the occasions when rival businesses have joined forces to prevent government legislation from affecting their practices.

Elsewhere, in the corporate world, I've seen missions take place in which peaceful resolutions haven't been considered during tactical planning, usually in company restructuring processes. A large company decides to streamline its infrastructure and it invades the relevant departments – sometimes literally. Teams are broken up and new practices are implemented without discussion. There are casualties: members of staff are laid off. In those situations, the arising conflicts and reprisals can be demoralising and long term. Trust in and loyalty towards the company are blown away. (Especially if, as a lot of restructuring companies tend to do, promises are made that it will be 'business as usual', only for massive changes to take place.) The remaining members of staff look for an escape route to another job.

However, when restructuring is executed with a peaceful resolution in mind, the results are often energising Honooty breeds trust and loyalty. The future looks bright for everybody involved because the workforce feel safe and trusted. As a result, they become emotionally engaged. Meanwhile, the smaller actions are just as powerful as the grand gestures. I once worked for a firm that was subjected to a takeover. New faces came in every day to watch our operating procedures. One time, while working at my desk, I felt a tap on my shoulder. Some guy I had never seen before was staring at my computer screen.

'What are you working on?' he said.

It was an aggressive move. There were no pleasantries or introductions, and straight away I became defensive. I barely gave him the answers he needed: a small conflict had been created between us. But had he introduced himself with a smile and a handshake, I would have felt at ease. He would have found intel much more forthcoming from me. After all, diplomacy is often the best tactic.

THE INTEL

- Remember: when facing conflict, *we* are the gatekeepers of our emotions and actions. We are the ones who choose whether to become angry and aggressive or friendly and engaging, nobody else. That fact is a vital tool when readying ourselves for a potential conflict.

  So, say a colleague unfairly blames for you a mistake at work. You might flare up and lose your temper, causing an ugly clash; the time spent arguing and the subsequent communication breakdown might reduce productivity and affect team harmony. The safer option would be to refocus – breathe, recalibrate, deliver. Once you've gathered your thoughts, you'll find it much easier to explain yourself from a calmer standpoint and resolve the dispute.

- Slow the situation down. If it looks as if a problem might be reaching flashpoint, take a step back. Keep your gestures calm and speak slowly and quietly. If we're relaxed in our mannerisms, there's a very good chance the person we're communicating with will mirror them. People tend to feel silly if they're bubbling over while others are in control of themselves.

- Consider the intricacies of our body language. Entire books have been written on this subject, but potential flashpoints are usually resolved well in advance by a combination of engaging behaviour and some well-chosen words. Meanwhile, we should always be aware of the signals we give off as individuals and as a group. Often it's very easy to make an unintentionally aggressive move – the way we walk, a bone-crunching handshake, an offhand comment – that ends up creating a conflict we hadn't intended.

  During that potential flashpoint in Baghdad, the guys I had been working with weren't looking to attack. In fact, they were doing the opposite: they were defending themselves. But the manner in which they did it – rolling through towns in an armoured vehicle that bristled with artillery – came across as aggressive posturing. It upset the locals. They felt intimidated and threatened. That's why it's important we step outside of ourselves during moments of potential dispute to check for anything that could be misconstrued as confrontational. As I had proved that day, it can be vital in heading towards a peaceful resolution.

- We should always focus on the positive aspects of any mission when approaching a conflict. So, say we were to become embroiled in a dispute with a colleague while working towards a common goal: keep the overall objective in mind, rather than point scoring or trying to win a petty feud. It will help you to achieve your long-term objectives more effectively.

16

HANDLING THE DIRTY WORK

Decision-making can be an upsetting process. With responsibility come some tough choices. Business leaders have to make personnel cuts; sports managers have to drop players. In the family home, financial changes during hard times can lead to disruption. How often do we hear of people having to move their kids out of schools during a recession or give up family holidays and other luxuries? In the Special Forces, our tough decisions can sometimes involve losing colleagues or killing enemy targets, and it's never pleasant. These choices can be emotional, destabilising and disturbing. But how best can we handle them?

COLIN: Sometimes in the Special Forces we are called upon to execute an unpleasant task, one that makes us feel uncomfortable, even though we know its success is imperative for the greater good.

The same occurs in life outside the military world, too. All of us have probably been tasked with doing something that, for one reason or another, we'd rather not do. It could be that we've had to sack somebody at the office or break some bad news to a client. These decisions haven't been made without thought: they have to be implemented. *They're for the greater good.* How we deal with working through those moments is what defines us as leaders.

Weirdly, those types of decisions are easier to make when you are in a conflict because we can wrap up the consequences in a fairy tale setting: doing something nasty in a theatre of war can save hundreds, maybe thousands, of lives in the future. That's what we tell ourselves when we suffer collateral damage or kill one or more enemy targets. So, for example, during a hostage rescue raid, I was part of a team that rescued all the captives but lost a man along the way. (You can read more about that particular mission in the 'Teamwork, Leadership and Responsibility' section of the book.) That was bad news, but overall the mission had been a success; we captured the ringleader of the group responsible, which was vital for our intelligence and future missions. It doesn't make life easy, however. I've made decisions in the past that have killed people. The results of decision-making are far more brutal in a conflict when lives are at stake.

In the civilian world, the stakes aren't as harsh, but our perspective on painful gains is very similar. At times, a leader might have to delegate unpleasant procedures, such as changes they know will upset their team. In a business setting this could include the rethinking of a popular working practice or the introduction of staff cuts that will save the company thousands of pounds in the long run and secure the future of the remaining personnel. These decisions usually produce emotion and uproar, even though the far-reaching gains are rewarding. Psychologically, we have to accept the costs and move forward positively.

THE INTEL

None of us are equipped to deal with the emotional consequences of our unpleasant decisions. We're human. We have feelings. Luckily, civilian life throws up situations that are admittedly less grisly than war, though they can be emotionally harrowing in other ways. *Picture a situation where we've been forced to lay someone off as a part of sweeping redundancies. We're close to that person in the office. We know their family. We understand their financial situation – the pressure of mortgage and loan repayments. The decision to let them go will inevitably entail sadness and guilt. It's a tough call to make.*

But there's a reason we've been charged with orchestrating such a drastic change: we're leaders, and it's part of our responsibility to do the dirty work, whether we like it or not. That decision has been made for the greater good of the company. Of course, should we disagree with the morals of our position, we can always disobey orders. We can put up a fight or give someone else the job. Though, next time, it might be us on the receiving end of some difficult decisions.

Nobody said being a leader was easy.

17
HOW TO LEAVE A MAN BEHIND

In most walks of life, losing a colleague is considered a tragedy, a nightmare (which it is), but in the Special Forces it's all part of the package. That's why a mission is never considered a disaster just because somebody has copped a bullet along the way. But it's a very different debrief altogether if every hostage in an extraction mission has been executed or a high-profile target manages to escape in a high-threat detention operation. That's when serious questions are asked, and, as far as excuses go, 'We were looking after a wounded soldier' doesn't cut it. A fallen teammate shouldn't hamper progress during a mission. It should be the same in business, too.

ANT: So what happened when a soldier went down during contact? If the injury wasn't life-threatening, we'd patch the wound up as best we could, quickly moving the casualty to shelter or cover of some kind. After that, HQ – the support team that followed every mission and included a Sergeant-Major, primary fires operator and medic – would pick him up for extraction. I was once on a mission where a soldier fell into a manhole while trying to duck away from fire. The impact snapped his leg in two and he was unable to move. In those situations it was fairly painless to call in HQ for support, while pushing on with the mission. Well, painless for us. I'm sure the casualty thought differently at the time.

It was just as straightforward whenever a teammate got seriously hurt. We remained professional; there was no time to pamper any casualties if they had been shot in the neck or chest. Apart from the team medics, none of us were trauma experts, although we had been trained to stop the bleeding from a nasty wound and stabilise an injury before moving forward. In those circumstances we would take a minute or two at the most to perform a patch-up job and put the casualty into hard cover, but that was it. (If they were seriously wounded, one of the guys might stay with them until the medics arrived, leaving the others to push forward, and once that was done they would get back into the mix.) Taking any longer would lead to vital momentum being lost, the mission had to continue. It sounds brutal, but all of us understood the deal when we signed up for the job, it's the way we worked. Ordinarily, none of us would think about a casualty's well-being until after our extraction had taken place.

Obviously, it could feel more personal if a teammate was killed in action – or KIA – but regardless of who had been hit, our procedures remained exactly the same. We would always extract our dead when the mission was complete, though, but for us as 'door kickers' our missions were too important for any sentimentality, or emotion, to creep in. We had to get a job done, so whenever I was in a shit storm – two minutes, two hours, *two days* – I always zoned out, focusing on the task at hand. Once I'd returned to base, put my weapon down and had a wet on the go, then I'd allow myself some time to let the events sink in, but not for long.

Sometimes missions are abandoned. I've known a situation in which a building had been rigged up to the eyeballs. Several bombs went off like a daisy chain, killing a four-man patrol in the process. During those events, we usually evacuated any remaining soldiers on the ground, dropping the compound with an air strike before picking through whatever debris was left at the end for intel.

THE INTEL

You're probably wondering how all of this applies to civilian leadership. And, sure, we're talking in extremes here. However, these same principles apply to everyday scenarios, especially when teamwork comes into play, because in life screw-ups take place; bad things happen.

- *Your boss has gone down sick just as an important project hits deadline day?* Move on. Complete the mission.
- *The star player in your pub side has picked up a serious injury on the eve of a cup final?* Move on. Complete the mission.
- *Staff cuts are made in a car factory during a large-scale production run?* Move on. Complete the mission.

Most situations can be dealt with once sentimentality or emotion has been stripped away. Without those feelings, a person can operate more effectively. It sounds harsh, I know, but often it's the only way to get a job done once things have gone horribly wrong.

18

LEARNING WHEN TO RETREAT

Often it can be hard to retreat from a challenging situation. Our pride takes over and we don't want to back down. But sometimes, moving away from conflict is the smartest way out, especially if it allows us to fight another day. How often have you heard the phrase about losing the battle but winning the war? This concept applies to civilian life as much as it does the military.

COLIN: Sometimes you know when it's time to retreat. It starts with a gut feeling most of the time, a general sense that we're about to get our arses kicked in a big way, and I've been there on a number of occasions. During the last Gulf War, one of the Special Forces' tasks was to clear a small outpost positioned to the north-west of Baghdad. It had been one of the escape routes out of the capital when the invasion first started. Saddam and his heavyweight personnel had flown through the area as the Coalition forces attacked from the south. I was part of a task force that was sent in to make sure that there were no defences in place. It was our job to destroy anything we found.

There was only one bridge into the area, a long structure about seven kilometres short of the town. We approached under cover of darkness, but what we didn't know was that the structure was being heavily defended. When our first vehicle moved across, the sky lit up with a heavy burst of Directional Finding, which is when the range of bullets and mortar shells has been worked out in advance, just in case of a surprise attack. That meant that as soon as anyone crossed the bridge, the Iraqi forces were able to open fire quickly and effectively.

The first round was a wake-up call. Although it was launched from seven kilometres away, it landed only 50 metres from our lead vehicle. Bullets soon peppered us from all over. The assault was so immediate and accurate that we knew we wouldn't be able to sustain our attack on the town, and that meant we had to make an immediate call: did the cons outweigh the pros? In this case, all of us were going to get killed if we proceeded with our mission. The shout went out for us to retreat.

At once, every vehicle spun and raced out of range. The

Iraqi mortar fire trailed us all the way. They even had an anti-aircraft gun that had been aimed at ground level so it could fire at advancing infantry. When I looked from my window, I saw our cars spanning out and flooring it in different directions. Bullets ricocheted off their armoured exteriors with a *Ping! Ping! Ping!* sound. It was like a scene from the cartoon show *Wacky Races* and, weirdly, I was laughing my arse off, even though a round might have taken me out at any second. Miraculously, none of us were killed.

God knows how.

All of us can be exposed to unexpected aggression, but how we react is what usually defines our levels of success in a situation when we've been ambushed or outnumbered. In that outpost, we were unexpectedly attacked – and with force. Had we known about the heavy protection in the town, we would have approached our target in a different way. The minute we realised we were out of our depth, we immediately retreated in order to rethink our strategy. There was no delay or hesitation. That would have seen us acting like sitting ducks Meanwhile, we knew that sticking to our original plan and racing headlong into a hail of bullets would have ended in mass casualties and very few tactical positives. We made the decision to run and got out of there as quickly as we could.

THE INTEL

This mindset would be well used in civilian life, though for a lot of us it's a struggle to even consider retreat. Our pride is dented; our egos see it as failure. *For example, we might spend too much money when buying a house because the thought of losing it to somebody else is too much to bear; we chase a bad bet at the bookie's in order to recoup our losses; we take on a work project that's beyond us in an attempt to impress our superiors, or we attack a senior colleague in a heated meeting because we want to prove ourselves.* Pride can be a dangerous adversary.

More often than not, these situations end with a chastening and messy defeat. Meanwhile, our failures can prove psychologically damaging. I later experienced similar disappointments when working on hostage rescue missions in Iraq and Sierra Leone. Our team would land in a location only to find that the people we were after had moved – sometimes hours or even minutes earlier. It could be a miserable feeling loading back onto the chopper, empty-handed. The trick, I discovered, was to turn that low into a high and I found I could do that by following three simple steps.

1. RECOGNISE WHEN TO BACK AWAY

In any conflict where factors might be getting beyond our control, we should always ask one question: do the risks outweigh the advantages of success? In military terms, that could be the fact that we might lose too many key soldiers for us to be able to complete our long-term goals. In the civilian world, it could be that our mission is set to fail. However, is pressing ahead going to be detrimental to our career, reputation, health or finances? If the answer is yes, then retreat. *Live to fight another day.*

2. FIND THE HUMOUR IN DEFEAT

It doesn't help to get angry after a loss. It's counterproductive to lash out or sulk. That's one of the reasons why alpha male characters struggle to make it through the Selection process: their egos won't allow them to back down when sometimes a retreat or pause for thought is the first step towards long-term success. Instead their pride forces them to rush headlong into more trouble. The Special Forces know it's far better to slow the situation down, before withdrawing and regrouping.

I didn't drive away from that situation in Iraq ranting and raving in frustration. I didn't turn around and attack again in a blind rage. Instead, I laughed at our predicament because it was the best way of processing the disappointment in those early stages. Believe me: we have a dark sense of humour in the Special Forces. If a teammate – a good footballer, say – had been shot in the leg during that mission, none of us would have dwelled on their bad luck afterwards. More than likely someone might have made a crack about his team looking for a new penalty-taker next season. We're put in dangerous situations, where the risk of death is high, with every mission, but the tolerance for failure is low. An inbuilt sense of humour is vital.

3. REMEMBER YOUR HUMILITY

Why? Because it teaches us never to underestimate an opponent or challenge. How often do we hear people complain about bad luck, poor timing and a host of other factors when talking about their latest retreat? It's a defence mechanism that helps us to process an unpleasant situation, but ultimately it's counterproductive. Once we've accepted that we've been beaten by the better team, individual or challenge, we can regroup and face up to the reality of what's needed to be successful next time around.

Humility also prevents us from underestimating an enemy. An example of this would be a hostage rescue mission I was once involved in. As a group, the hijackers we were attacking weren't a military force. They were undisciplined. They were on drugs and booze and carrying AK-47s. In fact, they were more like a gang than an army. That should have put us in a position of confidence. But we were roping in from helicopters as a small team and were greatly outnumbered. At some point in the mission, all of us would be working alone, and while our enemy were operating at an inferior level, they were always going to have an edge in some way: they knew the local terrain, they had greater numbers than us; they might even have extra weaponry. Meanwhile, it didn't matter how good we were, if they had killed just one of the hostages during the mission, our work would have been considered a failure. Humility kept us sharp and focused throughout.

4. LEARN. LEARN. THEN LEARN SOME MORE.

As we've mentioned previously, defeat and failure are an opportunity to grow. So as a Special Forces unit will pore over their mistakes in the debrief process, so you should apply that to your life, too. *How did a project fail? Why did you not get past the first job interview? How did a long-term client come to choose another supplier? Understand and analyse your shortcomings and then grow from them.*

19

THE TACTICAL VALUE OF DEFEAT

We all take a beating at one time or another, whether it's while working as individuals or as a team. Sometimes a task we thought was manageable becomes too tricky and we later have to ask for help. (Those weekend DIY projects spring to mind here.) On other occasions we end up being beaten by another group or organisation when pitching for new business. The key is to spin a positive outcome from these negative situations; to take something from a loss, which is exactly what the SAS or SBS do after a blown operation, when something hasn't gone to plan or an Immediate Action changes the game completely.

COLIN: In Iraq, we would often work from the 'Playing Cards' – a pack of 55 cards giving the identity of the important enemy targets we were required to capture in a high-threat detention operation. Because the people listed were of such high value, they were very well guarded and tactically mobile. Often we would receive intelligence about where somebody was located only to find our objective had moved on.

In those situations it was key to react positively. So, rather than heading home with our tails between our legs, we would raid the compound for intelligence, because grabbing discarded mobile phones or computers could sometimes throw up leads. We would even talk to the locals in the area to see if anyone could be turned as an informant, while gathering information on how the enemy had defended their base with booby traps and IEDs. Those were the little scraps of victory that could be taken from a defeat and often those details helped us further along in the campaign.

Meanwhile, retreat, or the occasional pretence that we were beaten or withdrawing, was also used to lull our enemy into a false sense of security. Sometimes a tactic – for any army – is to encourage the enemy to attack by showing a false position of weakness. For example, in some situations we would draw disorganised enemy militia onto us, and once they had swept into view, guns firing, we would make an obvious show of retreating over the ridge as if running away in fright.

But it would be a trap.

We knew their troops were undisciplined. Whenever they attacked, they would lose all sense of order and tended to operate like headless chickens, especially if they sensed victory. Once we had spotted their squadrons racing towards us and made our 'retreat', their cars would break off and they would lose their cohesion. In their heads, they were about to make an easy kill and their gunmen were eager to shoot as many people as possible. But as they moved up the high ground, we would sweep over the top, hitting them with heavy armoury from above. Seeing us rushing across the terrain, and with strength in numbers, was often psychologically debilitating for them.

THE INTEL

- Pretending that we're in a position of weakness is a great method when hoping to surprise an enemy, in any situation. It can lull our opponents into a false sense of security, which encourages them to relax.

  It might be that we're negotiating a deal. Making out that we're tired, stressed and out of our depth (when, really, everything is under control), while conceding several inconsequential contractual points, is usually enough to breed over-confidence and complacency in the people sat across the table. Riding over the hill, all guns blazing, during the final minutes to secure the strategic factors we require – metaphorically speaking – can strike a powerful psychological blow and result in victory.

- Never waste a moment of failure. Take every chance to learn from your mistakes and gather information regarding where you went wrong and where you need to be stronger in the future. *If you missed out on a job opportunity, for example, try to discover the areas where you failed, and work on them. Don't sulk, or feel sorry for yourself. Instead, take as much value from defeat as you can. Use it to your advantage.*

20
REMOVE THE FEAR
OF FAILURE

As we've already mentioned, success is defined very
differently in the Special Forces. In any other public-service
industry such as the police or fire brigade, death and serious
injury within a team environment would be considered
a failure. For the SAS or SBS it's regarded as collateral
damage and to be expected. Likewise, when we capture
a high-profile target, there's no party or awards ceremony
afterwards. Instead, we just carry on, business as usual.
That sounds screwed up, but it's part and parcel of the job.

Despite the expendability of its operatives, there's
a loyalty that runs through the Special Forces, from top
to bottom. A lot of that stems from the debrief process, in

which rank is put to one side in order to gain an honest,
360-degree perspective. It's here that our successes and
failures are analysed, and we use different parameters
to measure them: we never punish honest mistakes or
celebrate great results. As a result, the fear of failure
diminishes.

Civilian leaders could learn a great deal from our
processes . . .

FOXY: In the civilian world, when a project goes well or a task has been successfully completed, there's a tendency to celebrate. *Woo-hoo! High fives all round! Everything's great! Let's move on!* If something goes horribly wrong, there's an inquest; we apportion blame. Scapegoats are hunted down. *That was shit. Whose fault was that? Get rid of them – fast.* It can all be very knee-jerk.

But what are the psychological results of that attitude? Distrust and anxiety, most probably. People come to sense they are under threat, especially when they're made to feel insecure and their livelihoods are put at risk following a cock-up. As a result they find it harder to perform to the best of their ability. Loyalty to the organisation can suffer, too.

Success and failure are treated very differently in the Special Forces. If we screwed up a high-threat detention mission and a target got away, nobody was sacked or had wages docked from their pay packet. We would look at what went wrong instead. We discussed where we could have improved.

Commanding officers understood that every member of the Special Forces is an elite soldier; they have all passed Selection. Mistakes are mistakes and as long as each individual has the presence of mind to want to be a better soldier, there is no point in shit-canning them.

Meanwhile, there was always an understanding that no botched job was completely negative – something could always be gleaned from a failed operation. There was always intelligence that could be gathered about how the enemy liked to set up or the weapons systems they used; somebody might have discovered a computer hard drive in the back of a compound or amassed some intel from people on the ground. The information gathered could prove vital in future missions and cock-ups were generally treated as part of the learning curve.

The same thing happened when a mission ran smoothly. We might be given a congratulatory slap on the back when returning to base, but nothing more. After that we would treat the debrief session in exactly the same way: we'd run through the lessons learned and analyse the new intel we had picked up along the way. The Special Forces' identical approach to success and failure bred confidence because we were learning all the time and nobody was going to lose their job over a cock-up. The guys above us had our backs. We repaid them with loyalty and an unwavering desire to succeed.

THE INTEL

- Don't freak out at failure. Bring your team together and learn from the mistakes made as a group. Encourage the people in your care to educate themselves from the intel gathered.
- We make mistakes. Be sympathetic to team members who might have messed up. Your understanding will breed loyalty. Of course, should they be serial offenders you might want to take a different approach!
- Don't waste success. Soak up every new piece of intel and use it to your advantage next time around.

21
HOW NOT TO BLOW VICTORY

Sometimes success can be as damaging as defeat. If that sounds weird, consider this: how often has a major result in business caused an outbreak of complacency or greed? (Clue: a fair bit.) How often do we see successful sports teams being stung by too much self-belief when facing an inferior opponent? (Again: more than we should, especially when it's the England football team.) As in defeat, we can glean plenty of lessons from victory. The trick is to make sure we make a habit of looking for them.

FOXY: You'd be surprised at how many people blow victory, and it usually happens in one of two ways. The first is for complacency to creep in. A mission goes by easily, almost too easily. Suddenly we allow our guard to drop; we relax. Then something knocks us off guard, robbing us of any tactical advantages that we might have gained.

The second is that we get greedy. We think, 'I've hit my targets, why not get a bit extra?' We try squeezing more from our achievements than we should. *As a result of our success, we find ourselves in demand; we're tempted take on more work than we can handle, or ask for more money than we should.* This tends to happen when we're on a success high, but it can be a recipe for disaster. At best we might get into a situation where we're scoffing more than we can chew. But the nightmare scenario is to become completely overwhelmed. *Taking on more work crushes us with fatigue; asking for more money earmarks us as being greedy or unrealistic.*

That's when the shit usually hits the fan.

I've experienced that exact scenario during conflict. I was in Afghanistan hunting down key Taliban figures with the Special Forces when we received intel that somebody we were looking for was hiding in a nearby village. We located his building and stormed the place. Our man was apprehended after a brief firefight, alongside another key target, which was a result: it meant we could extract further information from them in the future. We also discovered a weapons cache brimming with explosives and rocket-propelled grenades.

The mission had gone off without a hitch. But while we

were rounding up our prisoners, I heard a kerfuffle behind us. Two Taliban gunmen were legging it from the building. Now, nine times out of ten, 'squirters' like that are just farmers armed with AK-47s. *Small fry.* They're generally harmless and most of the time we allow them to scarper, even though they're enemy fighters, but this time we gave chase. Soon we were racing into the far yonder, through a field of god-knows-what. Our completed mission had been over-complicated and we were suddenly vulnerable.

Talk about a shit show. Prior to landing on the village we had assessed all the locational intel. I had developed a good understanding of where we were approaching from; we knew exactly where we had to go and we had all our access points planned out. Our instructions couldn't have been clearer. We were supposed to drop in, detain our target, and move on. Now we were running into areas that hadn't been checked in advance. And while there were air assets above us, nobody was able to deliver any real assistance because we were moving into uncharted territory – it was too confusing.

Then it got noisy.

A bullet whipped past my head. I didn't have a clue where I was as I moved in and out of compounds, trying to locate the two gunmen. But I was aware our unit had been overstretched in the chaos. Then the call came through on the radio: 'Time to leave.'

A chopper was called in, and as it landed my team protected it with bursts of covering fire. We had come into the Taliban's backyard, grabbing two prisoners. Unsurprisingly, they were pissed off. Now their forces were fighting back. Once we were away, we realised we had overstretched ourselves. Nobody had died, but there could have been serious implications.

Instead of cheering our successes back at the base we were counting ourselves lucky that our greed hadn't cost us.

We should have got the hell out.

We had finished the mission. Our aim had been reached mega-quickly. Then we became cocky, complacent and greedy. We made rash decisions rather than stopping for a few moments to take stock of the situation. Had we drawn breath, one of us might have decided, 'Lads, we've got what we came for – let's forget those squirters and quit while we're ahead.'

Hindsight's a wonderful thing, isn't it?

I've found that missions tended to operate a lot more sensibly when the odds were stacked against us. I was once in a very high-profile hostage rescue in a team that was massively outnumbered by enemy fighters. Casualties were expected on our side. We went in and only lost one guy, but as soon as we had a hand on our man, we were extracted. We acted more cautiously, and therefore more effectively. Because the odds weren't in our favour, we didn't allow any room for complacency. We went in, did the job and scarpered. Game over.

THE INTEL

- Take stock. Once you've executed your mission, assess your situation immediately. Ask yourself: do you really need to do more? Is taking on that extra deal, or chasing more money, actually going to help? Stay in control.

People sometimes fall into that trap when they start their own businesses. Contract offers or freelance commissions start to roll in. To get off to a good start they accept everything, but it's only once they've seen the workload ahead that they realise they've bitten off more than they can chew. They become stretched, they can't operate effectively, and rather than executing half a dozen briefs perfectly, they find themselves completing double that, but not as well, thus hindering their chances of repeat business in the long run.

- Remind yourself of the danger of complacency. Just because you've been successful in completing a mission, it doesn't mean you're out of danger's reach. Steady yourself. Remain focused and alert. Who knows when the bullets might fly again?

- Conserve your energy for the next battle. I've seen what happens when people push too hard in the military and overwork themselves. In the short term, it drags soldiers into sketchy situations. Long term, it grinds people down. In the American military, troops would complete tours of Afghanistan lasting 24 months. They would go home for two weeks' holiday and then head out again. They were rinsed. They didn't get any rest time. Once they had got back into the game again, they were still exhausted.

It's the same at work: we can always do more. There's always an option to stay at the desk for a little bit longer.

But, ultimately, we have to switch off at some point, otherwise we're not going to recover effectively for the next day.

Once you've finished a project, draw a line underneath it. Move on. There's another mission on its way.

- Beware the ego. Victory feels great. It boosts our confidence and powers our ego. It says, 'You're the bollocks, mate, you nailed that easily. *You can do more . . .*'

We've learned in the Special Forces that carrying an ego can be counterproductive, which is why we place so much importance on the concept of the 'Grey Man', someone who can blend into any situation and is quietly confident. (For more on that, see Chapter 30.)

There's no place for the headstrong egomaniac; someone who doesn't take a situation into account effectively; a glory-hunter. The Special Forces tend to piss people off in their home patch during operations, so we have to be humble and respectful of the fact that (a) they're going to come back at us, and (b) they know the lie of the land better than we do, which gives them an advantage.

Once we've done our work, it's best to put the ego to one side. Remember the brief and call it a day. Pushing for extra might create more trouble than we're expecting.

PART FOUR
TEAMWORK, LEADERSHIP AND RESPONSIBILTY

INTRODUCTION

Everyone is expected to lead in the SAS and SBS, and most soldiers will have shown strong leadership qualities while working their way through Selection; it's an attribute the watching DS are searching for. Why? Well, the Special Forces function within extreme circumstances. Strong leaders across the Regiment are vital. Should one unit lose their Commanding Officer to injury or death in the field of combat, another individual can step into the breach quite comfortably, enabling them to complete their mission as planned.

By the same token, everyone in the Special Forces is expected to be a team player. Egotists, the selfish, reckless hotheads: none of these characters work effectively at the military's highest level because they tend to cause issues within a group working under heavy pressure. The ideal candidate on Selection is one that can fit in with a group and work to instructions, while displaying leadership qualities whenever necessary.

Not all of us are born to be leaders, however; taking charge in any job or civilian situation can bring unique stresses. Likewise, some people find it difficult to work within a team structure. In this chapter we'll deal with those very issues. We'll reveal the techniques used when working with a new unit for the first time, tips on how to deal with problem characters within a group, as well motivational measures for yourself and those around you when the chips are down.

OLLIE: The responsibilities I'd taken on by joining the military hit me on my first day as a Royal Marine. I was 18 and enjoying the glories of passing one of the toughest training pro-grammes going. I'd received my green beret and was keen to replicate some of the amazing adventures I'd seen in the Army magazines that could be found lying around the mess hall. You only had to flick through the pages to see pictures of grinning soldiers lifting the British flag in newly secured compounds or posing proudly in front of an armoured vehicle, guns raised in the air. It looked amazing.

I couldn't have been more wrong about the realities of conflict, though. My first tour of duty was an eye-opener: I was still wet behind the ears when I was sent to Northern Ireland during the 'Troubles', the war with the Irish Republican Army that took place in the last four decades of the twentieth century. Soldiers were being attacked from every quarter by paramilitary forces. It was a bloody conflict, and I got my first taste of what was in store as soon as I landed – *literally*.

Our squadron was touching down at an Army base in South Armagh, but as we slowed on the runway, a huge explosion went off at a nearby checkpoint. It was the IRA. They had received intelligence that we were coming into the area; apparently their plan had been to deliver a welcoming present for at least four fresh-faced Marines who were supposed to be manning that particular post. Luckily for me and my teammates, their intel had been wrong and, instead, the outgoing guard caught the full brunt of a 500lb car bomb.

We were immediately installed as the Quick Reaction Force, or QRF, and moved to the checkpoint in choppers. When we arrived, the compound had been blown to bits, the sky was black with smoke, and the ground was littered with debris and body parts. In the middle of it all was a burnt-out car, though it was more twisted metal than anything else.

My Sergeant had been in this situation on a number of occasions previously. Once we were away from the helicopter, he ordered us to pick our way through the wreckage.

'Right, lads,' he shouted, kicking a blackened steel helmet towards us. 'The first thing we have to do is see if we can find any of these.'

At first, I couldn't work out what the hell he was on about. *Why did he want us to gather up a bunch of tin hats?* Then I understood the grisly truth. As the helmet flipped over, I clocked the head – it was still strapped inside. Locating every skull, every face, was our way of officially identifying the dead. Within seconds of my first tour I had learned a grim lesson: military life wasn't the same as a photograph in some

Army magazine. This wasn't a game. Life in the Marines was *proper.*

I had grown up in a heartbeat.

Comprehending the responsibilities I now had – to myself and my team, not to mention the lives of countless innocent people – was a big deal. Once I had moved into the Special Forces, that sense of responsibility became magnified even more, because the stakes were suddenly so much higher. I was working on operations where the cost of failure could be disastrous. I was utilising weapons systems worth millions of pounds. There were even times when I was working under extreme pressure and lives were at my mercy. For example, it would have been horribly easy to blow up a whole village with a tiny technical mistake when calling in an air strike. That was a major stress.

But we were built to withstand that pressure. After all, that's why we were in the Special Forces in the first place, and when it came to mental robustness we were the very best and all of us were natural leaders. Sure, there are designated team commanders in the SAS and SBS, but all of us were more than qualified to drive from the front. As a result, the concept of teamwork within the Special Forces was incredibly powerful – it still is. I've never seen anything like it: it's usually seamless, and on certain missions a unit could function without communicating, which is something I've experienced a number of times, especially when working with the SBS.

When I went on dive missions we would work in unison throughout, silently moving through our tasks and executing our individual roles from the Mission Success Cycle. All of us were so well trained that we knew our successes didn't hinge on verbal communication. The most important thing, however, was an undeniable sense of trust. Respect couldn't be earned between operatives, often because there wasn't enough time. On some missions a team of four who had never met before could be thrown together in an instant, and it would be their job to instantly hit the ground running. During those missions there was no need to talk about CVs or experience. There was the understanding between us that we were the elite. We had passed Selection, therefore we were equals and could be trusted.

Within each team, all of us had been trained to an expert level, we could all fight to a high standard and all of us were team leaders-in-waiting, capable of swapping around should our commander go down. Meanwhile, anyone of us could lead from the back should the angle of attack change when we were pinned down during a firefight.

The good news is that all of these leadership concepts are transferrable to the civilian world. The bad is that not everybody is born a leader, not everybody can handle intense responsibility, and not all of us are capable of getting the most out of a team. Still, we can all show strong leadership by uti-lising the techniques detailed over the following pages. Take them on board and you'll soon find that working in a team – as leader or a key member of it – will seem much easier.

22

ESTABLISHING COMMAND

Establishing leadership within a new team can be tricky at the best of times. When you're pinned down in a ditch with enemy fire coming at you from all angles, it's even harder. But that's what we have to do on SAS operations when a new team leader is working with soldiers they might never have met before.

It's the same for new leaders in the civilian sphere; there are risks and pitfalls everywhere. Say we've landed a job where we're expected to inspire a team of strangers. Some of them might be waiting for us to trip up (especially if our position is coveted by one or two members in the

group), others might feel demoralised by the departure
of our predecessor. It's vital to start strongly and inspire
respect if our new colleagues are to fall in line quickly.
    Here's how to do it . . .

COLIN: As Ollie explained in the previous chapter, it's
easy for us to respect one another in the Special Forces
because we've been through Selection. Our elite soldier status
can't be challenged. However, we ship all sorts of characters
into the Regiment and some of them might be bad apples. As
a team leader it's imperative that we stamp our authority upon
them as quickly as possible.

   Leadership is an individual characteristic, and it can
be delivered in an endless number of ways. Some traits are
common with all leaders, such as the ability to deliver clear
instructions and make decisions quickly and effectively. Others
depend on the characters of the people in charge. Many management figures like to lead by example, others scream and
shout at the people working with them. In some cases, strong
leaders are able to understand which of their team members
will benefit from high praise and those that might shrink from
instructions or gestures that seem aggressive.

   Change can bring positive results, too, which is something we see with football managers all the time. A new face
comes in and suddenly players who were performing to only
60 per cent of their ability for the previous boss are playing to
their maximum. When it comes to varying leadership methods,

the SAS is no different to any other job, in that there are no set styles. We don't instruct from a handbook. The only requisite is that team leaders have to ensure their teams perform to 100 per cent of their ability at all times, not just when a change in command takes place.

Taking ownership of an unfamiliar group is a challenging experience. However, the quickest route to successfully galvanising your assets is to invest in the group both emotionally and physically. Emotionally, the first step is to reinforce the value of the team members. All of us have perceived values within a group − it's why we're involved in the first place. For example, a banker will have certain skills that make them valuable. The same goes for an estate agent, massage therapist or landscape gardener.

In the Special Forces, I always gathered my guys together in a meeting before missions and explained their individual values − both to the success of our operation and to me. So, say we were primed to blow up an enemy-controlled bridge in Iraq. I might be in charge of a demolition man, a linguist and a medic. I would go through the team one by one, reminding them of their individual skills and importance, while creating an understanding that we were all very much working as a team.

'Look, you're our demolitions guy,' I'd say. 'We're going to need you if we're blowing that bridge up, so if you need anything, let us know. We're your team and we're here to help you. Likewise, medic, I know there's a lot of kit to carry, so instead of carrying it all around yourself, maybe you want to run a little course and teach us a few bits and bobs on the basics and we can carry that stuff. Linguist: are there any key phrases we should all memorise in advance to make your life easier?' And so on. Immediately, the whole team was emotionally engaged.

As a new leader, it also helps to acknowledge a weakness in ourselves and then delegate its management to someone who might be more adept in that area. It recognises someone else's strength and creates a sense of trust. I always did that whenever an operation involved water. I could swim, but I wasn't the greatest swimmer, and in the Special Forces we had a lot of guys who worked in the SBS. For those operations, I would entrust a water-orientated skill to someone who was more experienced. I'd explain: 'We're parachuting in and swimming onto this boat. The chances are I'm not going to be fast, so maybe don't give me the knife, even though I'm the commander – who's our strongest swimmer? You have it.'

Physically, it's important we get our hands dirty as quickly as possible, too. Why? Because nothing increases loyalty quicker than watching a leader taking on a challenge, especially one we didn't fancy for ourselves. Meanwhile, a leader who grunts orders from the back without taking on any difficult roles for himself will quickly lose respect and authority.

In combat terms, never be the person who says, 'Look, we've got some incoming fire. Can one of you stand up and just run across to that tree and see where the bullets are coming from?' Instead, be the person who says, 'Guys, put down some covering rounds because I'm going to run over to that tree. While I'm running, keep a look out for where the bullets are being fired from.' You'll only need to prove yourself like that once. From that point on, your team should be fully engaged in your ability and the group's objectives.

Generally the quickest way to command immediate respect in the scenarios I've mentioned above is to establish a bond through personal communication – though this isn't always about being likeable. I've been on plenty of operations with Commanding Officers that I haven't liked on a personal basis, but they've opened themselves up on an emotional and physical level. They said, 'Listen, lads, this is me. Here are our strengths. Here are my weaknesses. Let's play off the strong points within this team and control the weaker elements . . .'

I trusted people like that with my life. I also found that, when the going got tough, that understanding was the most effective way to get the most out of any team.

THE INTEL

When leading a new team, we should run through the following steps:

- Acknowledge them as a group and express your confidence in their combined expertise. Establish your work as a team effort and explain that support is on offer for each individual. *So, for example, say you are the new manager of a landscape garden company and are meeting your team for the first time. You should express what impressed you in their previous work. You should point out the strengths and achievements of the group, while detailing how you would like to build upon the successes.*

- Meet with them individually and make them aware of your trust in their individual abilities. *Why is the company's production manager so valuable? What strengths does your accountant bring to the table? And which gardeners have a keen eye for design?*

- Create a level of trust by delegating to the team an element of the job that you might be less skilled to take on. *If, say, you are unfamiliar with the plant suppliers in the area, you should utilise a member of your staff who understands those relationships better.*

- Lead by example. Take on a tricky, and unpleasant task. Prove to the team that you're willing to get your hands dirty if required. *In this case literally. You should grab your shovel and muck in on a particularly physical task on your first project.*

23
HANDLING RESPONSIBILITY

Responsibility is scary in the Special Forces, mainly because the stakes are so high, though we've come to understand and accept the pressures in our line of work. It's scary in the civilian world, too, where extra obligations can heap unexpected and unpleasant stresses on all of us. Managing that responsibility and stepping up to the challenge are rewarding experiences, however. The first move towards success is to focus on the positives and make the negatives work for you ...

FOXY: I was drip-fed responsibility while serving with the Royal Marines, but once I'd joined the SBS, it was shovelled upon me big time. I was immediately made an Optics Rep. Sadly I wasn't put in charge of the vodka and whisky stash, but instead I was accountable for all the optical equipment used by the Regiment, which included NVGs and gun scopes. When I looked at the inventory details for the first time, I noticed that the combined value was the equivalent of an OK Premier League footballer, and I was in charge of the lot.

No pressure, then.

My role back then was also to ensure our optics armoury performed at the highest level. So if there was an advance in binocular technology, or a new gadget came out, it was my job to give that piece of equipment a trial run. If I figured, 'Yeah, this stuff's up to scratch', then we would bring it on board. But handling all of those tasks was a big deal, and at times I wished they'd picked Joe Bloggs over me.

'Bloody hell, am I in over my head here?' I thought on day one.

For the first few weeks there was stress. I was accountable for all the kit while it was in the storage units and I had to make sure that everything was signed in and out. If somebody had lost their NVGs during a mission, I didn't want to be the one getting blamed, so the role soon taught me how to be diligent and methodical. But it also showed me how to handle responsibility, particularly during those moments when I was worried about being out of my depth. It wasn't long before I felt totally comfortable in my new surroundings. I became adept at my job.

FEAR CAN BE AN ASSET – USE IT

We've all been there: new job, new role and new responsibilities. That brings pressure. Fear. But we shouldn't run away. Instead, we can thrive on it. I felt that same stress when I was made Optics Rep for the Special Forces, but I've also experienced it in a gunfight, and I managed both situations in an identical fashion.

That might sound weird, but let me explain.

Fear is an emotion that a lot of people consider to be negative – but it's not. It keeps us focused, and if we can control it, it allows us to execute the job in hand and survive. If we can't, fear becomes detrimental. We lose our heads. We go into a flat spin and that can become contagious. There's nothing worse than being in a firefight, or another already stressful situation, when a member of the team starts to panic. Suddenly everybody else starts to flap, too.

One example of this was when I was pinned down by the enemy in a ditch in Afghanistan (as mentioned in Chapter 5). I remember we were working on a hostage rescue mission when the helicopter my unit were flying in came under attack. It was night-time, I had NVGs on, but suddenly the whole sky exploded with light. Bullets ricocheted around the place. I saw rocket-propelled grenades coming up at us, tracer fire, too. We were in the shit. When I looked down, I noticed that I was gripping the knee of the bloke next to me; he was gripping mine.

Once we hit the ground I dived into a ditch. We were

mixed up in a heavy gunfight and it was messy. As I lay there, bullets *zing-zing-zinging* over my head, I thought about home. *I wanted to be with my mum.* But that sensation didn't last for long and within seconds, I'd acknowledged the emotion was there and accepted its presence. I knew I had to control my anxiety, otherwise there was a good chance that I and everybody else might get killed if I started to panic; my fear could spread to the others. Instead I used the emotion to sharpen my resolve.

'Hang on a minute,' I thought. 'I'm terrified but that means I'm still alive and in with a chance. I've been in this situation before and survived . . . Let's get on with the task in hand.'

I began firing back.

It's the same when somebody in a new job feels the strain. They freak out and make mistakes, and everybody around them has to pick up the pieces. For example, I could have been a similar situation in the Optics room, but I turned the stress of my newfound responsibility on its head; I worked on staying calm. Besides, flapping would only affect the people around me. Instead, I used my experience to flip myself into survival mode. It was enough for me to shoulder the responsibility and drive forward.

'I'M HERE FOR A REASON.'

Generally, when we're given responsibility it's for a reason. Somebody, somewhere, has seen value in us, and the work that we've done in the past. But whether we're the CEO of a multinational company or a cleaner working for said CEO, every now and then we'll encounter a situation that seems unmanageable.

The cleaner might walk into a room that's absolutely trashed. It's massive in size – *a shit show*. The CEO might be in a situation where they've lost a multimillion-pound deal. The whole company was relying on it in order to attract more investors – *another shit show*. In both cases, the cleaner and the CEO freak out. But really there's not a lot of difference between them: in those moments, it's vital they remind themselves of their value. They've been entrusted with responsibility because of their skills and experience. And now it's time to step up.

It was the same for me. Once I'd managed the fear of my responsibility as the Optics Rep and reminded myself of the value my Commanding Officer had placed on my ability, I switched on. I realised that they weren't going to put any old idiot in charge of a room full of highly valued equipment. They had chosen me because they knew I could do it. The realisation fired me up and I was soon performing to the best of my abilities. The effects were exponential, too.

'I'm learning about something and I feel empowered,' I thought. 'Now I've got a purpose in this unit.'

SLOW THE SITUATION DOWN

Sometimes reminding ourselves of our own worth isn't enough: responsibility can be thrown at us because there's no one else around. We become accidental leaders, and that can be stressful.

During Season One of *SAS: Who Dares Wins* we heaped responsibility onto a couple of the volunteers during an Immediate Action – a CASEVAC in which four people carried a 'wounded' teammate. A designated leader navigated them through the woods to a safe meeting place. On every occasion we placed one of the weaker members of the group in charge.

This was done for three reasons: (1) to show that everybody has to step up in the Special Forces at times, usually when a team leader has been injured or killed; (2) to expose those who were unable to take responsibility; (3) to prove to those who thought they were unable to take responsibility that they were actually capable of pushing beyond their limits.

Some of the guys took to it quite easily, but one volunteer, Mark Fisher – no. 04, a personal trainer – crumbled under the pressure. His team was soon led into trouble and as the man they were carrying began to weigh them down, a few of Mark's teammates questioned his judgement. I could see that Mark was a decent dude, but he didn't have any confidence in himself. He became flustered and made rash decisions. There were disputes. Mark was eventually reduced to the role of lead scout (and a poor one, too) as the rest of his team took over, and in the end they became lost. It was a disaster. The pressure of responsibilty broke Mark and reduced him to tears.

'I'm not a good leader,' he complained. 'I knew that would happen.'

I reminded him of why he was there. After all, Mark

had stayed strong on previous days when several others had dropped out. Had he been able to do that for himself, he could have steadied his mind. *Breathe. Recalibrate. Deliver.* In an instant he could have slowed the situation down, taken stock of his value and shouldered responsibility. I guarantee you his decisions would have been delivered with confidence shortly afterwards.

USE THE PEOPLE AROUND YOU

Mark's team was an asset, but he failed to recognise that fact. Instead, he allowed them to become a psychological hindrance. His control was relinquished as he made a series of hasty decisions and incorrect choices. The stress of being in charge overwhelmed him. Intead, he should have recognised that acting as team leader meant he had a bunch of blokes at his disposal. They were there to help. After all, good leaders know that they can't – and shouldn't – do everything. At best, that tactic creates stress and fatigue. At worst, it can endanger a mission. It's far better to recognise the skills and strengths in those around us and utilise them effectively.

I think Mark thought he would look weak by admitting his inexperience, but there's no harm in asking for help, even when we're in a position of responsibility. Just because we're in charge, it doesn't mean we're supposed to know *everything*. So, in that situation, Mark should have addressed the team as soon as he sensed trouble. He could have said, 'Right, let's slow the situation down. What are we looking at doing? Does anyone know about moving over this sort of ground better than I do? If you do, give me some ideas.'

That wouldn't have been a display of weakness. Rather, it would have shown he was savvy and aware of the resources at his disposal, which is a strong leadership quality. Once he'd gathered all the information from his team, he would have been in a position to take responsibility.

THE INTEL

When wobbling under the pressure of responsibility, we should remind ourselves of the following:

- We have been given the responsibility for a good reason: usually it's something to do with our talent and experience. *Let's say you are a gym manager, stepping into the role for the first time. You should reassure yourself that you were selected because of your previous experience and achievements; other people have noticed your abilities and value them. That should be enough to quell any self-doubts and insecurities.*
- Accept the fear. *A healthy level of anxiety will keep you alert.*
- If the handing over of responsibility was unexpected or inappropriate, use your fear to maintain focus. See it as a challenge, a chance to shine and improve. *At the very least it might give you some intel on how to prepare for the rest of your career as a gym manager.*

- Always slow the situation down in times of stress. And if things look as if they might become hairy, ask your team-mates for intel and support. *There might be people in the gym who have a better handle on the accounts set-up than you; some staff might have experience in inducting new members or dealing with customer complaints. All the available assets should be utilised.*

24

HOW TO MOTIVATE YOURSELF, AND OTHERS, AGAINST THE ODDS

Some jobs seem impossible. A jumbled scrap heap of receipts that need to be filed for the company's annual tax return, for example. A deadline that requires late shifts, lunch 'al desko' and weekend all-nighters (no, not the good kind). Or what about that looming deadline that has to be met in order to keep the business afloat?

No wonder some people just get up and quit.

Resigning isn't an Immediate Action plan for the SAS. We can't put our hands up in the middle of a firefight and shout, 'All right lads, I'm done . . . Off home now!' Giving up for us usually results in death or capture – neither of which is particularly pleasant. That doesn't mean we're impervious to crushed morale, though. We can hit the wall, too. But a Special Forces soldier has learned how to draw on the untapped mental reserves that might take him towards the finishing line in one piece. Well, just about.

COLIN: We were on a mission into the jungle to rescue hostages who had been attacked by a militia group. The prisoners were taken into a camp, where they were chained up, beaten and forced to endure several mock executions. It wasn't pretty, and after a period of failed negotiations with the British Army the Special Forces were sent in to rescue them.

Our commanders had expected heavy casualties from the mission and I could understand why. My unit's role was to head into the area, find the camp, and from a distance locate the hostages and the buildings they were being held in. We were then expected to wait in the jungle before helicopters arrived to finish the job. From there we were supposed to take out the sentries on guard and kill as many enemy forces as we could before the main attack group roped down from the choppers. Our boys would then would span out, neutralising the base and extracting the hostages.

The enemy were hardly well trained. They were rebels, and not experts like the SAS. They were also big on drinking and drugs. Their weapon of choice was the AK-47 and they were more akin to a gang than an army. Despite that, the odds were stacked against us. We were going to be outnumbered for starters. Some Special Forces troops were being roped down, which meant for a brief period of time they would be exposed to heavy gunfire from below. The enemy also knew the terrain very well, and there was a strong chance they might be more heavily armed than our intel believed.

Then there was the mission brief: no matter how well we performed, losing one hostage would have meant the operation was a failure, even if we had killed 100 per cent of the enemy. The pressure was on and the risks were high. Meanwhile, it seemed an impossible task and there was a good chance we would lose a number of men.

FIND YOUR INNER DRIVE

So what motivates a Special Forces soldier who has been tasked with working on a mission like that? For me, it was the thought of being the best at what I did and operating at the sharp end of a high-profile operation. For a lot of my time in the Special Forces that was my motivation. It gave me a buzz, even with the risk of death hanging over me.

People have often asked me whether I liked being involved in military conflict and the answer was always 'Yes.' It's true, too. I wanted to be a soldier and I saw going to war as fun. Being on attacks was exciting. I wasn't going on the operation because I was a Special Forces member and I had to. Instead, I saw it as my reason for being in the military: it defined me; I enjoyed being in firefights. Like most boys I'd picked up twigs and pretended to be at war from the age of five. The thought of being in combat for real got my adrenaline going, in the same way that people who jumped out of planes or climbed mountains got a rush of excitement. The only difference was that I had to pick up a gun and shoot people or rescue hostages.

I used that mindset to motivate myself on particularly dangerous missions. I also found that the responsibility of executing risky operations – those considered way too dangerous for the Green Army – was a powerful motivator. I used it to push myself during the most stressful situations.

EMPOWER THOSE AROUND YOU IN TIMES OF STRESS

I was the team leader in a group of five and we located the enemy camp quite easily. I reported back and informed headquarters of its layout, relaying the best attack points for our helicopters. But our approach had been hampered by the jungle's challenging terrain. The guerrillas had positioned themselves near to a fast-flowing river and we would be unable to get across without being spotted.

Pushing forward swiftly was tough. The primary forest around us was really thick and it was impossible to move through it at certain points. I knew the attack was going down in a matter of minutes, but the odds on us making it across in time, killing the sentries and neutralising any ground forces before the choppers had arrived were low. Our lads would have to fly in blind.

I called to the rest of the team and quickly outlined our situation. Time was running out, but I knew a clearer viewpoint on our predicament would be established as a group – any ideas and concerns could be quickly discussed. I found that in tricky situations it was better to have a team of guys who were willing to debate tactics than a bunch of sheep, happy to follow me into a hail of bullets. If somebody was able to come up with a great suggestion, I was happy to say, 'You know what, you're bang on. That's much better than what I had.' I felt it was a sign of strength because it showed self-confidence. It said to the others, 'I'm secure enough to take different ideas on board.'

These discussions also empowered the team on high-risk missions; everybody had a say in what our movements were set to be, and when it came to making a decision, the majority ruled. We were Thinking Soldiers rather than a group of individuals blindly following orders from a CO. Furthermore, when everybody is engaged in the decision-making process, there is a tendency for a group to discover a shared sense of motivation. Everybody operates at full throttle.

'Let's just swim across,' suggested one soldier.

I looked at the water. The current was powerful. We could end up at least a kilometre downstream before making it to the other side.

'Let's just fight through the primary jungle and hit the opposing camp and see what's there,' said another.

A couple of the group nodded. They initially wanted to

attack the enemy early, as our Direct Action had stated. I was tempted. But we were also tired, and when fatigue has set in, the temptation is to take the path of least resistance; to say, 'Let's just do it.' After all, it's less hassle not to argue. But I didn't want to make a wrong call by taking the easiest option. I hated the thought of a mission failing or losing a colleague because I hadn't been strong enough to stand by my convictions. Those mistakes can eat a person up for the rest of their life.

I outlined my fears for the outcome of the operation. 'An early attack carries risks,' I said. 'Because of the thick foliage, we might not get to the enemy camp in time. That's going to make our extraction impossible. Also, if we attempt to get across the river, there's a good chance we might get spotted or compromised. That's going to blow the surprise element of our raid and the whole mission along with it.

'We're then going to have to shoot our way out of trouble. Five against fifty: I don't fancy our chances. I say we wait to move forward, wait for the choppers to arrive and attack with them . . .'

The lads understood; everybody agreed on the plan. We crouched down by the river, frustrated. All of us were chomping at the bit to get involved. When missions go down, it's a great feeling to be at the spearhead, swooping in before the other components in a coordinated attack. On this occasion, however, we could see the bigger picture. For the greater good of the operation, we knew we had to stay put.

Weirdly, though, standing still is often the hardest move to make because it's passive. Saying, 'Let's attack first!' is much easier; it requires conviction. It's a positive move. And telling a Special Forces unit that they're not the first ones in takes some courage.

REMEMBER: NEGATIVITY IS CONTAGIOUS

Because our decision to wait had been made as a group, with our eyes on the mission's success, it meant we were able to remain focused. It would have been quite understandable had the group become demoralised. We had been hacking through the jungle for a while. The conditions were hot and knackering. The unit had been frustrated in our attempt to drive the mission.

As a leader in that situation, it's vital to be mindful of the consequences of our actions. I had four other blokes with me. All of us were under stress. But I had to remember that I was the face of motivation. I had to show inner strength. I had to inspire my team with confident decision-making and be a positive influence. Nobody was going to benefit from me sulking about the decision to stay put or moaning, 'I don't care I don't give a shit. It's a crappy mission. We shouldn't even be here in the first place.'

That attitude can echo throughout a team. Negativity spreads like a virus. If that happened, geeing up the unit once we were finally called into action would have been so much harder. But if I conveyed enthusiasm, determination and pos- itivity about our altered plan, my teammates were going to be more eager when it came to standing up at the starting line. They were going to attack the enemy with everything they had.

That proved to be the case, too. We worked our way through the jungle to the camp, and when the signal came to attack, we moved in with the helicopters. During the raid we rescued all the hostages, killing approximately fifty members of the guerrilla group and capturing their ringleader in the melee. We only suffered one fatality. When we were extracted and returned to our ship, I was told that command had expected to lose several men.

Against the odds, and thanks to a highly motivated force, our operation had been a major success.

THE INTEL

- Before any stressful or troublesome task, it's important we remind ourselves of our inspiration. For some of us that might be self-improvement, career development or even personal gain. Use the rewards of success as motivation.

- We should motivate our teammates by empowering them. Involve them during the planning phase and take their counsel on the decisions that directly involve them. They will feel valued and more fired up as a result.

- Remind them of the bigger picture. If our team is aware of what's at stake, it will help them to understand our decisions, particularly those with unfavourable outcomes.

- Remember: negativity can spread like a virus within a group faced with difficult tasks. As leaders, we must display positivity at all times. Remain calm and focused on the job. Be enthusiastic. The team should find motivation in our passion for a mission.

- Take motivation from failures. One aspect of the ethos of the SAS is the unrelenting pursuit of excellence, so our mindset would be to take the desolate feeling of potential defeat and use it as an advantage. Rather than dwelling on the negative outcomes, we would use our emotions as a motivational tool. We'd say, 'We've not been able to engage with the mission as planned. And that feeling we're experiencing now? It's not nice, so let's take everything we can from that and work doubly hard to make sure we never feel this way again.'

This tactic has been applied outside the Special Forces, and to great effect. During the 1999 Champions League Final, Manchester United were losing 1-0 to Bayern Munich. At half-time their manager, Sir Alex Ferguson, delivered one of his famous team talks as they regrouped in the dressing room.

'At the end of this game the Cup will be only six feet away from you, and you'll not even be able to touch it if we lose,' he said. 'And for many of you, that will be the closest you will ever get if we don't win tonight. Don't you dare come back in here without giving your all.'

United went on to win 2-1, scoring two goals in injury time. The fear of defeat drove them on to a spectacular victory.

25

'WHO BLEW THE WALL?' (HOW TO HANDLE A MISTAKE)

One thing that separates the elite soldier from a civilian operating at any level in the business world or in a team environment is the occasional disregard for responsibility. In the Special Forces, when we say we're going to do something, we do it. In the civilian world, that doesn't always seem to be the case.

It's a similar situation when it comes to the idea of admitting to mistakes. In business, at home or in life in general, if we screw up there can be a tendency to bluff. We shrug off our cock-ups; we pass the buck and blame others, or contributing factors, mainly because we can get away with it. In the Regiment, we take it head on. If somebody makes a mess of something, they'll raise their hand and 'fess up. We know it's the quickest route to self-improvement.

ANT: I retired from the Regiment in 2011 when a close mate of mine was killed in the Middle East due to the lack of responsibility shown by a local policeman. It had been a cock-up and I remember thinking at his funeral that I didn't want to work alongside people who acted like part-timers. I'd spent my career working with the best; I wanted that to continue. I also had a wife and two kids at home and I was keen to be around for the children as they grew up, so I decided to jack in the military life.

I moved into a more stable career when I had the opportunity to work as a security consultant in the African mining industry. Once installed, I applied the Special Forces ideals to my new job, which was a mistake. I was too trusting. Whenever somebody told me they were going to perform a certain task, I believed them. I expected them to do it. A lot of the time, I found myself feeling let down, because a form I had been told was completed actually remained unsigned or a simple job hadn't been finished. I was often frustrated because people weren't fulfilling their responsibilities.

I had been trained differently. If, as part of an SBS mission, I was due to enter a building via a hole that was being blown through a wall by one of our demos guys, I knew the job was going to get done. I wasn't going to arrive at the target and find a fully standing wall. As a result, I had the faith, 100 per cent of the time, that when I arrived at a compound as point man, I'd be able to step into the building and clear the room – that would be my only focus. I didn't have to spend any time worrying whether the explosives had worked or if the breaching team had got there in time. Because of our operational procedures and attention to detail, those tasks were going to be completed, bang on time. Unless something had gone horribly wrong and we had unexpectedly stepped into a firefight.

If only that was the case in the civilian world.

While working in the African mining industry, I'd often get to the hypothetical wall only to find it still standing. I'd have to spend time looking for an alternative access point, a door usually, and then wear myself out kicking the thing in, before walking into a room full of waiting gunmen. Too often in civilian life, I found myself working with amateurs. People promised to do things and then failed to deliver – even on the basic stuff. It held me up. It was even more frustrating when people told me what I *wanted* to hear, only to let me down afterwards. People would claim to be on top of something when they weren't, or close to completion on a certain task, only to be nowhere near. They were bluffing. That was something we never did in the Special Forces because it was so dangerous.

No bullshit, because it could end up costing someone, big time.

That's why I never try to play people now. If I'm in a meeting and things are going wrong, I won't try to talk my way out of a dodgy situation. I'd rather not engage in bluffing. And I definitely won't tell somebody something they're hoping to hear, not if it's untrue. Instead, if I'm asked a question I can't answer, I treat the situation in the same way that I used to treat a gunfight: I slow everything down. *Breathe. Recalibrate. Deliver.* I'll explain to everyone that I'm not sure and I don't want to pluck an answer out of the air that might be wrong (and cause complications for everybody as a result). But I'll make sure that I have the correct answer for them as soon as I get out of that meeting.

In the Special Forces, if we screw up, we admit it – it's the only way to learn from our mistakes. And, believe me, when we make mistakes, the consequences can sometimes be huge. One of us might let a suicide bomber through a checkpoint, having mistaken her for a mother carrying a baby. Somebody might have missed an IED while working through a protected compound only for it to detonate on our way out. On very rare occasions, somebody might have blown a hole in the wrong wall.

When it comes to our debrief sessions, however, that person isn't going to weasel their way out of it. Responsibility is taken. Lessons are learned. When I've applied that attitude to business people, they haven't liked it – not at first, anyway. They misinterpret my blunt answers for rudeness or arrogance, when actually it's honesty, and one of the best ways to move forward and learn. Only then can we progress in a team effort.

BOLLOCKINGS: HOW TO DELIVER THEM

How we utilise aggression in real life can define us as leaders. Ranting and raving works for some people, but it's unlikely to make us very popular. That style of management is fast going out of fashion, too. For example, football managers have used it in the past, infamously Sir Alex Ferguson, who was incredibly successful during his time in charge of Manchester United, but his style wasn't without collateral damage. Some players crumbled under 'the hairdryer treatment' – a torrent of rage where he screamed and shouted at his team in the dressing room if they had underperformed. A few others became embroiled in public disputes with him, most notably David Beckham, who eventually left the club for Real Madrid.

We hardly hear of that form of motivation in the game these days because in most environments it's understood to be debilitating. People become scared to make decisions or think for themselves; they become inhibited through fear. The shock value of attacks like that can wear off very quickly, too. If we're trying to rouse our staff or colleagues into raising their performance levels, a bollocking might work once or twice. After a while, though, everyone acclimatises. When the shouting starts the recipients are able to switch off.

'Here we go,' they think. 'Another rant. Just pretend to listen and it'll be over in a minute . . .'

Instead, I've learned that the best form of controlled aggression arrives with brutal honesty, something that's just as applicable in the civilian world. When I'm dishing out a bollocking to anyone, I remain calm and factual; I keep emotion out of it. I deliver the information in a steady tone of voice and most of all I try not to shout. (Though some of the recruits on *SAS: Who Dares Wins* will probably tell you otherwise.) I keep my head.

Overall, though, I remain truthful. If I've been let down by someone, I tell that person why they've failed and what they should have done. I explain why I feel aggrieved and what they need to do to rectify the situation. In the context of the SAS I knew that shouting at experienced and respected operators wasn't going to get me anywhere. Special Forces operators know when they've screwed up. They can tell by the intel delivered during the debrief – whether that be a target still on the loose, a dead teammate or several executed hostages. Screaming at them isn't going to salvage the mission. It's the same in an office – you have to ask yourself: what will I achieve by raising my voice? If it's because you want to vent your frustration, then it probably isn't the best course of action.

My style of bollocking can make people feel uncomfortable. They walk away feeling like they've been bullied or scolded, but it's a damn sight better than being shouted at. Most of all it's a productive and positive tactic. Nine times out of ten, if that person is a team player and in tune with the goals of your leadership, they'll understand. Hopefully, they'll learn from it, too. If that sounds harsh, well, that's because I come from a background where one mistake can cost lives. I've had to learn to use my aggression in a controlled manner. It's the only way I could perform with a clear head.

THE INTEL

- No bullshit. No excuses. Do your job. Admit to your mistakes.
- When dealing with somebody who might have screwed up, take a measured approach. Aggression is a tool, but we should only turn it on when absolutely required.
- Acting wildly, without thought, means we've lost control. Calm down before the situation gets out of hand.
- Overuse of aggression can result in diminishing returns – our actions may backfire on us.
- Practise controlled aggression: brutal honesty rather than anger; measured decisions instead of reckless actions.

26
THE BATTLE OF EGO

Ego can be destructive in a warzone. It tells a person they know better than their superiors and, at worst, encourages an individual to ignore orders. It causes people to act irrationally, especially in circumstances where patience or tactical acumen is required. It stops people from accepting defeat in a situation which they might walk away from to fight another day.

This personality trait can cause massive problems in the workplace, too. Individuals press ahead on tasks that are out of their jurisdiction; they make calls that aren't in their job descriptions because they want to impress a superior. Some people take offence at being asked to do a task they may feel is beneath them. They sulk and become disruptive.

With that in mind, it's vital that an egotist is made to work to the beat of the team's drum rather than the other way around. This might seem like an overwhelming challenge for any leader when attempting to work alongside a troublesome individual. But, as we've seen in SAS: Who Dares Wins, employing the right plan of action can sometimes reap long-term rewards.

OLLIE: A lot of us wanted to shake Jon Calloway when we first met him. A candidate from Season One of *SAS: Who Dares Wins*, he was an alpha male character, which isn't necessarily a bad trait to possess in the Special Forces, if controlled properly. But Jon couldn't keep it in check. (Though he wasn't the only one in the group who behaved that way.) He was arrogant and cocky; mouthy, rude and full of himself – at first.

In the gym at home, nobody could match him. Jon had the biggest guns. He probably got his pick of all the girls, too, so it came as no surprise to me to learn that he was a trainee stuntman. At one point in the show, he even told Colin that he fancied bettering the work of the Hollywood action star, Jason Statham. When he first arrived at base, he took one look at the competition and considered himself to be the top dog.

I think before I go any further it's important to stress that Jon is a changed character these days. So much so that he even helps out the lads and me when we're asked to appear at corporate presentations. On *SAS: Who Dares Wins*, however, he made a bad first impression and was very much on the back foot from day one. As far as the DS were concerned, his attitude made him a weak link. The Special Forces require people without ego, a soldier who can adapt to different situations and become humble at the drop of a hat; one who can communicate with people on all levels. That's because being grounded allows the SAS soldier to act like a chameleon in any given circumstances. It's no good getting captured and then giving it the big man in front of the guy holding a rifle. That attitude is the swiftest route to a bullet in the head. It might also result in an entire team being wiped out and a blown mission.

Jon struggled from the outset. He wanted to talk himself up in front of the DS, which allowed us to expose his weaknesses. It was clear from the beginning that he had a problem with authority, and he wanted to compete and battle with everybody, so we kicked that out of him as soon as we could. We pushed him physically and broke him mentally. Suddenly, he became very aware there was room for personal improvement. He was given a reality check, and by the end of those eight days we had turned him around. He probably thought, 'You know what? I might be able to curl 50kg in the gym, but my attitude is going to get me into trouble sooner or later. I would be a much better person with less ego . . .'

Eventually, he was one of only four candidates to make it to the end of the show. Sure, he wasn't the finished article, but we were able to prove that ego was Jon's biggest enemy because it brought him into unnecessary conflict with the people around him. That realisation taught him to rethink his attitude entirely.

ANT: We all encounter egotists in our day-to-day lives: a work colleague who wants to compete with everybody – all the time. The person in the office who believes they're better than the rest of the team, or somebody who seems determined to undermine authority. I know because, to a certain extent, I was that person.

Before joining the Marines and then the Special Forces, I wanted to prove myself to the world. I wanted my peers to know just how good I was. But rather than displaying it, I got to a point where I just didn't care. I knew I was better than them and I went out of my way to ignore people. It was childish and immature. It was only once I'd learned to focus on myself, my work, and my family and friends that I became capable of controlling my ego. It helped me to progress much quicker than before.

The problem with egotistical characters, in any team setting, is their potential to cause rot. They breed resentment and discontent. They undermine leadership values, so they have to be controlled. During the making of the show, I sussed Jon's character flaw once we started physically testing the group. I would tell them to perform a certain task and Jon would pull faces, as if my requests were beneath him or the challenges were too easy. His attitude stunk on those first few days. His body language suggested he was thinking, 'I know that already, why are you telling me this?' Or, 'What's the point in doing that?' In any walk of life, that attitude is problematic, especially if we're the person in charge. It questions our authority. It undermines us. Worst of all, it causes conflict and division within our group because before long, other people start to share the egotist's viewpoint.

In the field of combat, an ego can be very dangerous. Sometimes it can be better to retreat when pinned down by enemy fire. Outsmarting the opposition with brains is always the preferred option. Stepping back can be hard on the ego, however. It feels like failure. And if an operative has a tantrum and decides to run head first into a hail of bullets because they think they have a better plan or they're frustrated, it can be disastrous for everybody. Suddenly Immediate Actions come into play. Maybe CASEVACs, too. A tricky situation soon becomes a nightmare.

That rationale applies to civilian life as well. Plans and instructions are put in place for a reason, especially in work or on team projects. Should somebody decide to take a different path because of an out of control ego, or their desire to compete and rail against authority, it can screw an entire project. The challenge as leaders is to spot the big egos in our group and change them for the better.

THE INTEL

ANT: We turned around the egotists in *SAS: Who Dares Wins* fairly quickly with one simple technique. The DS led by example. We proved we were capable of handling challenges that were way beyond the egotist's skill sets.

Egotistical characters, in all walks of life, tend to think they know more. They believe they can do a superior job to the people above them in an established working system. One trick is to prove that they don't know better; that they can't always do a greater job, and the most effective way of getting that message across is to command their respect with a show of ability and experience.

During the first episode of the show, we ordered every recruit to complete a test run the SAS have long called the 'Fan Dance', a gruelling run across the Pen y Fan hill range. When undertaking this unpleasant exercise, every soldier has to carry a bergen on their back, stuffed with weights. To test the candidates' mental and physical strength further, the Fan Dance has to be completed within four hours. As the civilian volunteers set off, I understood from experience how gruelling a run it could be, but I wasn't going to sit on my laurels and watch from the sidelines, especially not with an egotist or two to break down.

As the recruits made their way along the path, Foxy set a fast pace, and I moved up and down the route, checking on the runners and their capability. Those that couldn't handle the speed were taken off. When it got to the turnaround point, I saw one guy running towards me. I knew he was super-confident, an egotist, so I decided to push him.

'You're not doing it any more,' I said.

He looked confused. 'Oh, why?'

'You're too slow. But I'll tell you what, if you keep up, then you can come back with me . . .'

I ran off, the guy close on my trail. He struggled, but he got to the bottom, though he couldn't make it back up and over to the finishing line, so I left him. I think that was the moment when he first realised that Selection was much harder than any CrossFit or Iron Man circuit he might have completed previously. The Fan Dance gave him a massive shock. Suddenly, he wasn't the top dog any more. The DS were. I had guessed that in that one guy's life, everybody looked up to him because of how he appeared and acted. But suddenly, he had stepped into *our* world. I had to show him that I knew exactly what I was doing, and that I was the best at what I did.

THE INTEL

Here's how you can make it work for you . . .

- If there's an egotist in your group then they shouldn't be hard to spot. Allowing them to act against the team and your leadership will become debilitating very quickly, so act decisively and command respect. Recognise their insecurity and work to help them through it discreetly. *So, say you work in a firm where presentations are key; your egotist is forever mocking the individual who has to stand up and talk. Why? Because you've sussed they suffer from insecurity problems. Encourage the egotist to make a presentation, so they can understand the challenges at first hand; put them on courses where they'll learn how to make company presentations for themselves. Turn their negativity into a positive.*
- If the egotist is coming for you, halt any challenges to

your authority by leading from the front. Take on a task that seems unpleasant or too challenging for the rest of the group.

- Should that fail to bring an ego into line, invite them onto a project where they will get to see your talents and experience in action at close hand, such as a company conference where you have a lot of responsibilities, or an event that showcases your authority.

27

DECOMPRESSION: THE VALUE OF UNWINDING

No rest, no rewards. It's a common complaint for a lot people in and out of the military. Most of us experience stress in our day-to-day lives, particularly those of us in intense jobs or family situations. It seems as if we finish one heavy project, only to start the next one almost immediately.

This punishing cycle can hit us hard. In the Special Forces, the nature of our work, and the rhythm of war, means there's very little time for rest or recovery. The fallout to a life spent in battle can be post-traumatic-stress disorder and burnout. Overworked people outside the military can

*be hit just as hard. A heavy load can lead to emotional
problems, breakdowns and illness.*

*When navigating these issues, the trick for any
leader is to understand the importance of 'decompression',
both for themselves and their team members. Meanwhile,
streamlining working practices and hitting the release valve
at the right time can reap surprising results.*

FOXY: Post-traumatic-stress disorder hit me hard. I did
too many tours; some of them were too close together and a
few of the skirmishes I got myself into had psychologically taken
their toll. I was affected by some of the people I'd killed, especially when the incidents had taken place in front of women and
children. I'm aware that part of our job was to exert violence,
but I was shocked at some of the firefights I'd got myself into.
After my final tour I felt detached.

At the time of my personal troubles, PTSD wasn't something the Special Forces had a grasp of. There was no doubt I
had been negatively affected by my work; a black cloud loomed
over me a lot of the time. But when I later went on a commander's course, an officer detailed the symptoms of PTSD during
a medical presentation. I laughed darkly to myself.

'Well, I tick a lot of *those* boxes . . .'

After a few months of heavy drinking and tearful episodes,
I went for help, but the Regiment had a catch-all treatment for
guys who were suffering from psychological problems. They
didn't realise that rehabilitation was an individual process,

and when a doctor asked me to recall the moment when I first might have experienced extreme stress, I knew I wasn't in the right place.

'The first time?' I thought. 'Mate, when *wasn't* I under stress? I ran the risk of being killed every single day.'

In the end I was medically discharged, but that didn't help because I felt ashamed at having to leave. I believed that I had much more to give at the highest level of the military. I told everybody who knew me that I'd quit because I'd contracted tinnitus, and deep down I felt lost. Leaving the Special Forces meant that I was cut off from my mates and my career. It took me a while to rediscover my inner focus.

COLIN: A day after being captured (see Chapter 14) and enduring several beatings and mock executions, I was back on the job, kicking in doors and looking for high-priority targets. There was no time for me to recover from the incident.

In the Special Forces, we worked hard. Because of the unrelenting nature of conflict, our operational cycle was very high; leave was very limited. If we were to slow up for just a second, the enemy might have got the drop on us. As a result, I never had the time to process what had happened to me on missions; there was no space to relax or recharge. For some people that might be a good thing – certain operatives might have struggled if given too much time to reflect. Personally, I don't know whether it worked for me or not. The jury's still out on that one.

Everybody needed to decompress, especially after a stressful tour of Afghanistan or Iraq, and we all unwind in different ways. Some Army guys like to drink heavily, but obviously that's not the answer. Other soldiers have outlets for their aggression– they might box or go to an Ultimate Fighting Club gym. A lot of people vent their mental stresses through adrenaline sports. They ride their motorbikes too fast or abseil down mountains. Then there are those people who like to talk about it, either to somebody who has experienced the same traumas as them or to a professional psychiatrist. Each to their own. Unfortunately, there isn't a template that fits everybody. What works for some people might fail for others.

The military world needs to reinvest in caring for its forces. Ordinary people have been placed in extraordinary circumstances and the toll has been drastic. We can't expect soldiers who have been under heavy fire for several years to just slip back into civilian life without any after-effects. They're just not on the same frequency as people who haven't experienced that life. They can't function to the best of their ability.

But just because the Special Forces work under incredibly tense and pressurised situations, we shouldn't think we hold the monopoly on stress. Everybody experiences it in their day-to-day lives; it appears in episodes in our home and working practices. A large number of people have been burnt out by working too hard, and, as leaders, we can sometimes push the people who work with us to breaking point, too. The key to successfully managing that situation is to develop an understanding of the concept of decompression.

Periods of rest and recovery following incredibly stressful projects or episodes can have benefits for our productivity and happiness, not to mention team harmony: how many times do you hear of punch-ups at Christmas parties? A company or business has one piss-up a year and after a few beers, all the little grudges and frustrations come to the surface. It can be like a lid blowing off a kettle sometimes. There are fistfights and arguments; team morale is shattered. But had there been regular periods of unwinding throughout the year – moments when a team can let off steam together – those ugly scenes might have been avoided.

MAKE TIME TO DECOMPRESS

COLIN: Too many corporate companies fail to recognise the benefits of decompression, but the issues are very easy to address. Good team leaders recognise the risk of fatigue, stress and low morale within their group. They react. They let the team share in the outcomes – good or bad – at the end of a project because that engages them with the process. Victory energises the group; defeat should inspire harder work, especially if everybody is committed to the team ethic (which is where bonding days out are so effective).

Finding the time to rest can encourage streamlining and efficiency, too. I recently came back from consulting with a big reinsurance company in Switzerland. They wanted Ollie and me to help reframe their business structure. Their aim: to become leaner, tighter, more brutal; fitter and stronger in their working practices. Inviting a couple of former Special Forces guys to assess their MO was an interesting step for them, but it turned out we were able to spot several flaws in their set-up. One of them involved decompression, or a lack thereof.

These guys were analysts. They were also perfectionists. What tended to happen was that they would be given six weeks to put in a proposal and they would instruct their team to take every hour of that six-week period to execute it. With the deadline approaching they would often ask for a two-week extension, wringing even greater effort out of their staff. But we could see their methodology was counterproductive. During the closing stages of a proposal phase, the employees became exhausted. They were unable to function to the best of their ability. When I spoke to some of the office staff, they painted a worrying picture.

'In terms of stress, we're working 16-hour days, some-times for a week or two before deadline, just to get these things in,' said one. 'Then nothing comes out at the back end – we don't even know if we've won or lost the proposal sometimes. We feel trapped'.

No rest. No reward. It was a worrying cycle that had demoralised a team unit, and their productivity was on a down-ward slope.

Ollie and myself recognised this flaw and ran an exercise with their key staff. We split the teams into four groups and asked them to solve a puzzle. Each team was given a different deadline – 20, 40, 60 and 80 minutes. All of them solved the problem within their allotted time, but all of them maxed out their deadlines, frantically dotting the *i*'s and crossing the *t*'s in the final minutes. They couldn't shake the habit of squeezing every last drop of time from a deadline.

We threw the results back at them. 'If you can do this effectively in 20 minutes, what's the value in spending 80? What's that extra time being used for? You're spending four times as long, when you could be focusing on other projects or improving the team and your practices.'

With one exercise they were immediately aware of how they could become time effective. Even better, they understood that everybody in the company could then enjoy a little extra time to decompress and unwind after a gruelling workload. When the next mission had come around, they were eager to attack again. They had learned from the mistakes of the military: no rest, and no respite, can lead to diminishing returns. Burnout follows soon after. And who benefits from that? Only our adversaries, most probably.

THE INTEL

- Inform your team of the results of their work at the end of a project. Success will energise them. Failure should act as a motivational tool – hopefully. Leaving them in the dark only creates frustration and fatigue.
- Can you streamline your working practices to allow time at the end of an operation? If so, utilise it!

- Decompression doesn't just allow us to rest and recover. It also gives us a perspective on our successes and failures. Reward your team with the opportunity to enjoy their triumphs and process the defeats.

PART FIVE
BECOME THE THINKING SOLDIER

INTRODUCTION

The difference between a standard soldier and the Special Forces is the way in which we think our way around a combat zone. For those of us who have worked in the SAS or SBS, it's not enough to follow instructions blindly. We have to adapt, plan, react and create, usually at a split second's notice. The ideal mission, as we've said before, isn't a bloody firefight where every single member of the enemy is wiped out in hail of bullets. It's the quiet extraction or hostage rescue mission, where we nail the brief without firing a round.

That's why we've been nicknamed the 'Thinking Soldier'.

In this section, we'll detail how that attitude can work for you. We'll teach you the ways in which your mind can push you through to the end of a seemingly impossible task, even when you're in serious pain, physically and mentally. We'll explain how you can operate as an army of one, shutting out the mental distractions around you while working towards an objective. And you'll begin to discover the opportunities available once you've mastered the concept of 'going grey', a trick a Thinking Soldier will use to blend into any environment, allowing him to work in a clandestine and effective fashion.

COLIN: For a Green soldier, life can be fairly simple. You generally do what you're told, no arguments – unless you want to be court-martialled, that is. Had I stayed on as a private or lance corporal during my military career my job would have been to follow the instructions of the bloke above me. I would have taken very little interest in the bigger picture during operations and my sole concern would have been whether I was following orders effectively.

In the Special Forces, we don't have that luxury. Soldiers have to think on their feet. They have to be able to react and adapt to the most minute of changes; we have to negotiate highly pressurised situations, such as capture and interrogation. The fact that we operate in harsh environments, where death can be the outcome of one mistake, means we have to rely on our mental strengths at all times. The SAS and SBS are more about brains than brawn. That's what makes us natural leaders.

All of us are highly trained in several key areas. For example, everybody in the Special Forces has a degree of medical skills, though one person on every mission will be a trained medic. It's the same for our weapons systems. All of us are generalists, rather than specialists, which is a major strength.

That's not the case with all military organisations. In other armies, such as the US Special Forces' Delta Force, or SEAL Team Six, soldiers are all specialists who have trained in one area, and only one. Their units will feature a gunner, a demolitionist and a medic. Medics will have studied for 18 months, and can deal with everything from tropical diseases to childbirth, but most other things, such as working as point man, are beyond them in a military capacity. Meanwhile, their colleagues are usually inexperienced in the medical field. Should a medic take a bullet during battle – a very possible scenario – the rest of their team would have to watch them bleed out fairly quickly. They would be powerless to save them.

Beyond that level of expertise, everybody in the British Special Forces has to think like a leader, and once we're on a mission the chain of command can become relatively loose. Yes, there's a designated team commander, but shared responsibility is key. There isn't one person barking orders as everybody else follows along, without thought. Instead, we're given a mission brief and on the ground we have free rein to make it work.

We're also flexible. We can decide to take one route, before switching to another should Plan A turn to shit. A unit might land on a target and decide instantly that their approach needs rethinking. When it comes to weapons, we don't have strict issue kit. We pick the best tools for the job from the armoury before leaving the base. Our ability is respected and we're trusted to think for ourselves in times of crisis.

One of the Special Forces' strengths comes from the fact that, when push comes to shove, we're all able to operate as leaders. Should our man in charge become a casualty, the mission won't fall apart at the seams; we won't suffer from a loss of momentum and there's rarely any squabbling, fear or conflict caused by a power vacuum opening up. Instead, one of the other guys on the team will step into the role, without fuss. Work then proceeds as planned. That's what sets us apart from other military units, and most civilian organisations.

In a corporate or civilian setting, it's quite common to see uncertainty break out whenever a team leader goes sick or becomes unable to lead for whatever reason. Without another natural leader to fill the void, people panic. Delay and bad decision-making hamper their work. Whenever former Special Forces personnel have presented leadership courses in a business setting, they've often been shocked at the chaos that follows should a figure of authority become incapacitated. If you don't believe me, look at the financial chaos that ensued once David Cameron announced his resignation in the aftermath of Brexit. The pound plummeted, which, in some small part, had a little to do with the mystery surrounding his replacement. Once Theresa May had been installed as British prime minister, the pound began to rally (though only for a little while).

One exercise performed by myself and the other lads speaking at corporate presentations is to 'kill' the leaders. We split a large group of staff members into teams and create a hostage rescue situation for them to negotiate. Immediately we ask for a volunteer from each group to act as leader. The usual suspects always put their hands up: the execs, board members and senior chiefs. It's a natural response. Those guys are used to doing it and they're expected to take responsibility during important decision-making processes.

Immediately, we take them out of the game. We give them a diminished role.

One of us will say, 'Right, Mr CEO, you're Headquarters. It's your job to act as a go-between. Every time your team comes up with a mission plan, you tell us what that plan is – nothing more.'

Disorder follows; the staff ordinarily operating below those natural leaders freak out. They don't know what to do or how to act. It can take a group ages to settle upon a leadership figure and decision-making becomes sloppy in the process. Even the basics, such as who should present a plan to the room, can result in squabbling. It's fun to add a little pressure by reminding the teams of just how many hostages have been executed while they've dillied and dallied.

This exercise is done in a gentle way, but it exposes a major flaw that can be found in most team settings: when it comes to major operations in any working environment, at times we have to act fast and become a leader. We have to think effectively. Failure to do so can result in disaster – especially during a conflict. But a lot of people haven't been given the skills to work that way. For example, the choice to take on responsibility comes from confidence. That confidence comes from education and expertise, which is within reach for all of us. Only understanding that can help us to become Thinking Soldiers.

However, one or two techniques might help you to get there a lot faster . . .

28

UNDERSTANDING AND OVERCOMING YOUR WEAKNESSES

*All of us have a weakness, there's no exception
to that. During the Selection process, soldiers will find
that the chinks in their armour are being exposed, and
quickly. It might be that somebody has an extreme
aversion to cold; there could be authority issues, a lack
of patience or the tendency to blow up angrily should
things go awry. Every individual on the course will hit a
low point due to their weaknesses. The key to survival is
preventing those flaws from affecting us negatively. And
the only way to do that is to learn about our negative*

traits, accepting their presence and managing the
problems whenever necessary.

FOXY: None of us are superhuman, and if we're unable to control the flaws within us, they can lead us to fail. The egotist will run headlong to their own death through machismo. The worrier will freeze in a ditch as rounds fly around them. The over-thinker will find it impossible to rely on their gut instinct or trust their decisions, when decisive action is vital. But the good news is that the Thinking Soldier can identify their weaknesses and learn from them. You can, too.

My problems were never too far from the surface: I was terrified of failure and it messed me up. It did my head in. I hated the idea of my reputation being tainted by a mistake I'd made, which would put pressure on me. That pressure would then cause me to make a mistake, meaning it had become a self-fulfilling prophecy. It was crazy, and that mindset only intensified once I'd joined the Special Forces because the stakes were raised. There was no room for error – *anywhere.*

Just after passing Selection my fear of failure caused me to screw up in the most embarrassing way, though luckily it didn't have any major implications because we were on a training drill. At the time, I was on a high. I was new into the Special Forces; I was one of 14 blokes to have passed from an initial crew of 350. I thought I was the dog's bollocks. Previously, when I was working elsewhere in the military, I was able to operate within my comfort zone. I had spent ten years in the Marines as a reconnaissance troop in one of the fighting units – it's the pinnacle of where a Marine wanted to be. I went into Selection thinking I was switched on, but within a week I felt out of my depth. It was that tough. When I later joined a Special Forces squadron full of experienced soldiers I thought, 'Oh my god, I'm just another minion and I'm still learning the ropes.'

We worked on training exercises in the beginning, and one day I was put into a two-squadron attack comprising 40 experienced soldiers. We were doing live firing, using explosives and shotguns; we were all dressed up in black with our balaclavas on, which was everything I wanted when I first applied for Selection. I thought, 'This is cool!' Then my mindset refocused on the people around me. The chink in my armour was exposed. I wanted to prove I was a switched-on soldier but my mind said, 'You're working with some serious professionals now; you'd better not screw this up.'

We were operating in darkness. A shout went out: 'Right, we're going to move on!' But I wasn't able to. I had re-bombed the shotgun, but it had jammed.

'Hold!' I shouted, which meant nobody was moving anywhere. I kept re-racking the ammo but it wasn't working. I started to panic; my fear of failure kicked in and I couldn't work out what the hell had gone wrong. The blokes around me became impatient.

'Let's go, Foxy. Let's go!'

'What the fuck's going on here?'

I tried to explain that I had a stoppage, which was

when a counterterrorist instructor stormed over, seriously annoyed.

'What the fuck's going on here?'

I waved the weapon around. 'There's something in this shotgun,' I said. 'It's fucked.'

The instructor grabbed the weapon and inspected the chamber. Then he pulled out the shotgun cartridge and scowled.

'Well, it would help if you put the rounds in the right way . . .'

I wanted the world to open up and swallow me whole. I was a new face, trying to prove myself, but I'd cocked up massively because I'd been frightened of losing face in front of a squadron of elite soldiers. I could hear the piss-taking flying around me. Everybody wanted to know who had messed up because we were all wearing balaclavas.

'Name and shame!'

'Who was it?'

'Foxy!'

'Who's Foxy? You absolute dick . . .'

To this day, I'm adamant that I hadn't really put the round in the wrong way. My guess is that there was something genuinely wrong with the gun, but the instructor decided to give me hell, just to keep me on my toes.

I had a real problem with failure. I kept beating myself up over any mistake, sometimes for a couple of days. I would screw up and then think, 'Fuck, I must be absolutely shit. I thought I was good, but I'm not . . .' It wasn't a new situation.

The instructors had even spotted it during Selection and they placed me in pressurised situations, just to see how I would react. One time, I was the lead scout on patrol and I missed an enemy target. Another lad in the unit spotted it, and we completed the mission, but afterwards the DS came down on me hard.

'Fox, you were the fucking lead scout, but you missed the target,' he shouted. 'You were supposed to be responsible for all these guys and the mission . . .'

After the shotgun incident, I was about to ready myself for another sleepless night of dissatisfaction and stress when I realised that making mistakes wasn't the biggest problem: not being able to handle them was a larger issue. In the Special Forces, they like you to accept screw-ups and move on. *No dwelling – there isn't time.* The system teaches us that we're all human and we make mistakes. What's important is the way in which we respond to those errors. I identified my flaw. Whenever I blundered, I told myself, 'Hang on a minute, you're a 26-year-old soldier: of course you're going to screw up. You just need to learn from the errors, and take those bollockings on the chin.'

From then on, I did my best to recognise my flaw. I told myself it was OK to make mistakes. I just had to learn from them, and move forward.

I never failed to re-bomb a shotgun ever again.

THE INTEL
Identify and manage your flaws

To know your weaknesses is actually a strength: it shows understanding and self-awareness. Write them down and identify the chinks in your armour. Ask yourself where you feel most uncomfortable and why? What tends to lead you into making mistakes? Then ask the people around you what they think your weak points are. Once you have recognised what you are doing wrong, start to work out how to improve upon it. Here are some examples:

- If you lose your temper when meetings don't go your way, learn how to slow the situation down (see Chapter 13).
- If you crumble when speaking in front of large groups, practise talking in front of mates, or volunteer to present in smaller crowds and then work your way up.
- In a working sense, you tend to rush to your own death; you make rash decisions – check yourself before every bold move: are you making the smart play or allowing your ego to run away with itself?

Remember, these flaws don't have to be permanent – they're ever changing and can be managed. You can work on them, with practice and in training. When you're approaching a situation where your flaws and fears might become exposed, ready yourself and handle the situation head on.

Understand the importance of humility

When somebody's weakness has been exposed in the Special Forces, it doesn't take too long for the jokes to begin – even when something really dark has happened. It's a defence mechanism. It stops us from dwelling on our mistakes, and turning an awful situation into an irreparable one. It also helps us to maintain perspective in a stressful situation. Make light of your situation – it will ease the emotional shock of failure.

Don't be too proud to ask for help

Once you've identified your weaknesses, redeploy your skill sets to help you manage those flaws. On a Special Forces operation we build a team according to the tasks ahead. Sometimes, however, skill sets might be missing due to a mission being organised at the last minute, or if an Immediate Action is coming into play.

If, for example, we were blowing up a compound wall to gain access, it's no good somebody with zero demolitions experience volunteering themselves for the explosives work. Instead they should explain their deficiencies in that area, and move into a position that suits them. Likewise, somebody shouldn't offer to enter into an urgent, deadline day negotiation for their company if they're indecisive and struggle to make snap judgements.

In the Special Forces we're taught that asking for help when it's needed is a sign of strength, not a weakness. It's no good if one of us doesn't really understand the map they're reading during a mission, especially when there are a few blokes alongside them who are more than capable of helping out. But it is irresponsible to pretend to understand what's going on when really you're bluffing while hoping that no one else notices. That type of behaviour is regarded as irresponsible.

Instead, make the most of the assets available. Everybody has a support network around them: friends, family, work colleagues. Have the confidence to say, 'I'm not sure what's going on here.' It could be the difference between success and failure. After all, far better to admit your weaknesses early on rather than have them bite you on the arse in the heat of the battle.

In the past, I've liked to encourage that idea. I've addressed a group and told them, 'Guys, the one thing we need to understand is, if someone's having a bad day, fucking look after him, because *you* could be having a bad day two weeks down the line. The bloke that you could have been giving shit to for being weak is actually the bloke that's holding you up.' Often, it's worked out that way, too.

29
HOW NOT TO QUIT

All of us have thought about quitting at one stage or another. The mental or physical hurdle in front of us seems insurmountable and we think, 'I can't do this, I'm off.' But the truth is, there's always more we can do, in any situation. A lot of the time, the brain or body is telling us that we're done, when, actually, we're nowhere near to breaking point. The trick is to reboot our internal setting, while tricking the mind into thinking we're working within our limits. It's a lot easier than you would think . . .

OLLIE: Towards the end of *SAS: Who Dares Wins* Season One, we offered the remaining recruits an opportunity to call home. There weren't many people left at that stage, and those that remained were physically exhausted. After enduring five days of brutal training on limited sleep, the majority had been mentally destroyed; they were emotionally vulnerable. In that moment, we were rewarding their hard graft with a brief reconnection to the outside world.

Well, that's what we led them to believe, anyway.

In reality, it was a trick. What we were really doing was delivering a test of resolve. One of man's greatest weaknesses is self-doubt. It's there in all of us to some degree or another and, once it has crept in, it acts like a rot, and one that's very difficult to rid yourself of. That link to the outside world, whereby one phone call connected them briefly to their partner or a family member, was enough to trigger the biggest self-doubt of all: *Why am I doing this?*

It became an interesting crossroads for the surviving applicants. Those guys who made the phone call visibly weakened. The ones who declined generally stayed strong. Among them was recruit no. 11, Ryan Roddy, a mixed-martial-arts fighter and one of only two people who made it to the very end. When I later asked him why he hadn't wanted to call his girlfriend, Ryan delivered the golden answer: 'Because I was scared it would cause me to lose focus.'

Ryan was spot on. There's no room for distractions on a Special Forces mission, big or small. Whenever I went on an operation, such as during the Northern Ireland conflict with the Marines in the 1990s, I always severed myself from the life back home. I knew it would otherwise have been a distraction.

Dealing with problems such as family disputes, weekend engagements or even plans to decorate the bedroom at home was only going to cause me to lose sight of the main objective. When the stakes are so high, as they are on all Special Forces missions, one slip in your concentration can prove fatal.

A Special Forces soldier can detach himself from the outside world quite easily. While hunting down an al-Qaeda chief in the mountains of Pakistan, he's unlikely to receive texts from mates inviting him to the pub. Most of the time, my friends and family didn't have a clue where I was because of the secretive nature of my work. That meant I didn't have any contact with home during missions, which was vital. Emotions attached to a more normal life are enough to create self-doubt and cause someone to think, 'Why am I doing this?'

That applies to the civilian world, too. How often do you see people struggling to reach their goals because of their personal difficulties? Real life tends to get in the way of everything. But severing personal ties is generally much harder away from the military. It's out of order to ignore phone calls from your partner for weeks on end, just because a big work project is nearing completion or if a fitness goal needs to be achieved. It's also unlikely you'll stay popular with mates if you're ignoring their texts for long periods of time, no matter how stressful a home redevelopment project has become. However, what you can do is tell your mates of your important project, inform your partner of the increased workload you're experiencing. Explain that you might have to withdraw slightly if you're to reach your goals.

Elsewhere, I would always visualise my prize at the end of a particularly gruelling mission. Whenever I was in the middle of a firefight and needed extra motivation, I always looked beyond the final goal. Rather than visualising the end target, the exact moment when our enemy had been neutralised or a mobile missile-launcher destroyed, I imagined a point beyond it: the rewards of our success. I'd fantasise about a night out with mates – loads of beers and a great meal. I'd picture an embrace from my girlfriend. Sometimes I would go even bigger and imagine the things I'd like to buy with my earnings – a beach holiday or a bigger house. I would see sun loungers on a beach, the cocktails and grilled lobster; I'd dream about what it would be like to sit in a bigger garden during the summer evenings.

It wasn't enough just to see these rewards. I found it helped to attach emotion to each fantasy, too. Picturing the night out or the sandy beach was great, but I had to *feel* the happiness of each situation, so in each picture I imagined myself smiling, laughing and having a great time. *I soaked up the happiness.* And once positive emotions had been attached to my fantasies, it created an extra incentive to complete whatever mission I was on at the time.

If you don't believe me, the next time you're asked to work through an arduous task in the office or during a tough physical activity, such as some heavy lifting at home or a gym class, picture how you're going to reward yourself afterwards. If you're drinking a few beers with mates in that moment, picture the scene, say it to yourself, over and over: 'Drinks with friends. Drinks with friends.' You'll be surprised at how quickly your focus shifts from the pain of whatever you're doing to the rewards, which act as a very powerful incentive.

This psychological technique has got me through some very testing times, when it would have been quite easy for me to lose my focus or to quit. My Selection for the Special Forces, for example, was a nightmare. I was in the middle of the Hills Phase, and I had been flying around the Brecon Beacons on a long run with a heavy bergen on my back. I was strong. I felt great. But just as I was reaching the finishing checkpoint, I turned my ankle at a 90-degree angle. There was a loud crack. All the tendons had ripped on one side and I was in agony. 'Fuck,' I thought, 'this could be the end of it.'

I hobbled to the bottom of the hill, and as I gingerly took my boot off, I saw one of the Directing Staff out of the corner of my eye. As he walked past me, he shook his head. Then he used his finger to draw an imaginary line across his throat, a sure sign that he believed I was done for. It was clear to me that everybody thought my Selection was over and, that evening, a training officer even took me to one side.

'Look, Ollerton, because of your injury we want to take you off the course,' he said.

I wasn't interested. As far as I was concerned, quitting wasn't an option. I didn't want to throw in the towel. I told him I wasn't giving in; I was continuing with the Selection process.

'Well, as long as you understand me,' he said. 'If something happens tomorrow, that's you never coming back.'

When I went to bed that night I was in serious pain, my

ankle had ballooned, and I knew we were scheduled for a massive yomp over the hills the next day. The next morning I necked a ton of painkillers and strapped myself up, but every step was excruciating; I was in tears. 'Fuck me, I've got six months of this,' I thought, but I knew that mental strength would get me through the agony, so I pictured the rewards at the end. I saw my celebrations after being passed in. I was with teammates, we were laughing; there was a real pride at becoming elite.

I was right, too: with my mental focus altered I managed to grind my way through the Hills Phase. Seeing beyond it had protected my focus and helped me to endure the pain.

COLIN: Like Ollie, one of my lowest points during the whole Selection process was on the Hills Phase. We were doing a point-to-point navigational assessment during the Test Week. I needed to get across some of the most brutal terrain on the whole of the Brecon Beacons, hitting checkpoints along the way, but I was in agony. The tendons had inflamed under my kneecaps and I was in a tremendous amount of pain. I did everything I could to keep the injury from my mind, but every step was agony. At times it was as if somebody was digging a chisel underneath my kneecap.

It would have been so easy for me to come off at that stage, the pain was so great. Even walking would have been a relief, especially with all the weight from the bergen strapped to my back, and the sturdy boots that I was wearing. But I knew that walking meant failure. I wouldn't reach the checkpoints in time. I just had to grit my teeth to get through it. It took a lot of mental strength to get around that day, which I did with the help of four mental primers.

1. I remembered my experiences

Before signing up for Selection, I had served in the Army for a while. I had experience, and I was considered an effective operator. Every time I began to feel the pain eating away at my knee and self-doubt began to creep in, I told myself that I had a right to be there. I reassured myself that I had it in me to complete the task. That experience – of having endured conflict, hardship and hellish conditions – meant that I was less likely to quit. I think my upbringing helped, too. I'd maybe had a rougher upbringing than some people, in which eating three meals a day wasn't always a given. In a way that might have made me less susceptible to quitting than someone who had enjoyed a more privileged childhood.

2. I eliminated the possibility of quitting as an option

I knew that if I went into Selection with the option of withdrawing at the back of my head, quitting would have been much easier. At times it would have been tempting to think, 'You know what? Any time, I can jump on the wagon, get back for a hot bath and a hot meal.' If I kept thinking about a Get Out of Jail Free Card, chances are, I was going to take it at some point.

3. I understood the potential for self-improvement through pain

Having convinced myself that the option to put my hand up and withdraw at any time didn't even exist, I told myself I was improving as a person just by being there, regardless of how painful or gruelling the workload was. I then soaked up every minute of the experience. I treated it as a massive lesson from start to finish. I knew that attitude would take me further. Even if a member of the DS had dragged me off the course at that point, I'd have gained enough experience to make something of my failure: I'd have truly understood my mental and physical capabilities.

4. I focused on my long-term future

I had a goal. I wanted to be in the Special Forces because I wanted to operate at the highest level. I had a hunger for self-improvement because I *needed* self-improvement.

Had I come from a more established position, taking on such a difficult challenge would have been much tougher. A city broker or a professional footballer earning £100k a week might find it far easier to quit a tricky task because their life is already full of luxury and excitement. I was a soldier. The thought of going back to Salisbury Plain, where I'd previously been getting wet and digging trenches for not very much money (and not being involved in the exciting missions executed by the Special Forces) was definitely a motivating factor.

THE SICKENER AND THE 40 PER CENT THEORY

FOXY: On day four of *SAS: Who Dares Wins* Season One, we brutalised the recruits by putting them through the Sickener – arguably one of the toughest tests on Selection. In short, it's a physical and mental grind, a series of punishing drills and exercises that won't let up until a predetermined number of individuals drop out through exhaustion (not that we tell them that). For hours the group ran up and down hills, submerged themselves in water, and did push-ups and sit-ups; they weren't allowed to stand still. Every time they believed the test might be coming to a close, we made them do something else. Not knowing when the day was going to end pushed the weak to the edge. I watched as people hobbled around in agony and puked their guts up. It's a horrible exercise.

Then we messed with their heads even more.

We allowed the recruits to think it was over and ordered them back to HQ for food. But just as they settled down to eat, we sent them out on another run, which was followed by a CASEVAC drill in which they had to carry a teammate up a steep hill in a fireman's carry. As their bodies began to tire, we mentally pounded them, over and over and over.

'Is that the best you have, number 26?'

'What the fuck are you doing here? Either you can do this or you can't . . .'

'We have to get rid of some dead wood. If you don't have the minerals . . . *withdraw*.'

Much of focus here was on who had the mental capacity

to battle through the pain barrier when they were at their lowest ebb. People who can't carry on working when there's no end in sight won't be able to handle being in a highly pressurised battle environment, because there are a lot of false endings during war. Just when you think a firefight might be over or a mission is coming to an end . . . *Bang!* You get hit again. On Selection, we need to see if people can handle that stress; we need to find the quitters. If you're not the sort of person who can keep pushing on while bullets are flying around and people are dying alongside you, you're not the sort of person who's going to fit in with the Special Forces.

But you can dig in. *Everyone can.*

Why? Because our brains are telling us porkies. People these days have become lazy; we want an easy life. Our bodies want to protect themselves. When we think we're at our limit, in any situation, our minds tell us that we can't take any more, that we're unable to continue, and that, if we do carry on, something bad might happen to us. In a physical sense, pain and fatigue overwhelm us. During a mental task, we might tell ourselves that we're too frazzled to go on. But we're not. There's more in the tank, we just have to dig deep if we're to find it.

The US Navy Seals have a theory that no matter how bad we feel or how tired we get, we're actually nowhere near the limit of what we can achieve; the brain is deceiving us to save the body from pain. In fact, they think we're only 60 per cent there. It's a way of saying that by drawing on our mental strength we can push through any situation. But talking percentages when our knee is throbbing, or there's a never-ending mountain of paperwork in sight and we've only had three hours of sleep because of our crying newborn kid at home, is hardly inspirational. When the chips are down, tell yourself you have at least 40 per cent left in the tank. Then, as Ollie said earlier, find a mental carrot, a reward, and see yourself living it.

Then drag yourself to it.

THE INTEL

- Quitting is not an option. Tell yourself that, anyway. You'll find it much harder to press the ejector seat button if the possibility isn't at the back of your mind. *That mind-numbing DIY job you have to do at the weekend? You can't quit. That final training run before a marathon? You can't quit. A never-ending research project at university? You can't quit.*
- When enduring a daunting task, think *beyond* the moment of completion. Don't see the finishing line, visualise the spoils you'll win by completing the task: the glass of wine at the end of the hard day; the party with friends; the slap-up meal and congratulations. Get vivid with your imagination – experience the sights, smells and tastes. See a picture of you living that moment, and see yourself smiling and laughing in it. Use that as your driving force.
- What's next? Use the benefits of completing your task as reminder of your motivation. If slaving through the night

to complete an important work brief is going to score you points at work, focus on the rewards: the kudos, the congratulations, and the possible promotion or bonus.

- When all else fails remember the 40 per cent theory. You're only 60 per cent done, whatever your brain is telling you, so picture the rewards at the end and get yourself there.

30

BECOMING THE GREY MAN: THE BENEFITS OF BLENDING IN

Becoming the 'Grey Man' is one of the key components of serving as a successful Special Forces operative. It's about being able to blend into any situation, by adapting our personality and actions, even our appearance. Our movements shouldn't alert the suspicions of the enemy and, if we've done our work effectively, walking through the homes of our aggressors, unnoticed, should come quite easily.

That chameleon quality is useful in life, too. It allows

us to blend into situations where we might not want to draw too much attention to ourselves. Someone starting a new job might want to retreat into the shadows a little so they can assess the nature of their new colleagues. It's a rare quality to possess naturally in life, however. It requires somebody to forget their ego; they need to act with humility, because showing off, or acting boldly, can be a tactical disadvantage. After all, it's far better to be underestimated by an enemy than overestimated.

COLIN: The reason we refer to this skill as being the Grey Man is because it's such a bland colour; grey is unremarkable and unmemorable, which is vital for anyone hoping to work on covert operations. If SAS soldiers were all 6 foot 4 inches in height and built like brick shithouses, it's unlikely our missions would get very far. Everybody would stand out as potential threats and we'd be identified very easily. In that respect, our line of work is unique. Making an impression on the people around you can lead to problems. Not standing out in any way is a bonus.

During the first season of *SAS: Who Dares Wins* a number of the volunteers looked the part on the opening day. They were bigger than a lot of their teammates. They were quicker, and more confident. But by the second episode several of them had dropped out. The guys who made it to the very end were mainly the ones who went unnoticed in the early stages. They possessed strength of character and the ability to adapt to any challenge thrown at them. Their humility later allowed them to negotiate their way out of trouble during an intense 12-hour interrogation phase in which they were psychologically broken down by various unpleasant methods, such as exposure to white noise.

The same thing happened to me throughout my Selection. During the Hills Phase I was never out front during the runs, nor was I at the back. Instead, I often found myself in the middle of the pack. There were a number of soldiers who seemed physically superior to me, but they couldn't go the distance mentally and eventually dropped out. When I finally passed into the Special Forces I was one of 12 successful recruits from an original pool of around 200. I remember one bloke coming up to me at the very end with a confused look on his face.

'Where were you?' he said. 'I don't even remember seeing you on Selection. In fact, I don't remember seeing you *anywhere*.'

I took that as a compliment. It meant that I had successfully blended into my surroundings. Nobody had been alerted to my presence, which meant I could slip into just about any situation unnoticed on a mission later on in my career. Those skills were quickly transferred to my life in the Special Forces. With the help of camouflage I've been able to go undetected in desert, urban and jungle terrains. Elsewhere, I've worn different disguises to blend into a variety of situations, even wearing coloured contact lenses and dyeing my hair. Those little details were the difference between operating undetected and standing out.

As the Grey Man I also needed to be adaptable. Sometimes I had to change my appearance unexpectedly because we were operating on the move. I've found myself starting surveillance in a city location wearing a suit and tie. I was able to move among the commuters without anyone giving me a second glance. When my plans had to change, I dashed through a supermarket, buying bits and pieces to alter my appearance, before tearing at my clothes and roughing myself up so that within minutes I resembled a homeless person. But this wasn't about dressing up or being like an actor. In the Special Forces we had to be flexible in order to react to the ever-changing situations we found ourselves in. Going undetected, even for a split second, might be the difference between getting caught, and so blowing a mission, and escaping.

It's not just our appearance and actions that make us 'grey', but our mentality, too. That's why people with inflated egos rarely pass Selection: their pride and aggressiveness cause them to fail on many levels. We have different shapes, sizes and looks coming into the Regiment. The key characteristic we all possess is that we're able to change our mindset without complaint or stress.

To do so, we sometimes have to tone down the more prominent aspects of our personality. For example, a Special Forces unit might get captured in battle. It would be understandable if one of the team members lashed out at their attackers in a rage: their ego needed them to fight back. Chances are, that's the first bloke to be shot when it comes to dishing out executions.

In a business context, a comparable scenario might be somebody meeting a group of clients they've just started working with. At times, retreating into the shadows a little could prove to be beneficial. Sure, they should remain personable, positive and friendly, but a slightly withdrawn position will allow them to observe the personalities of their new colleagues; they'll be in a position to spot social dynamics and see what the office politics are; and perhaps note some potential strengths and weaknesses that could serve as powerful intel in the future. However, being loud, brash and overconfident might lead them to expose their own flaws and foibles; they give too much of themselves away.

Good leaders possess that same skill. They're chameleons. They can adapt to different circumstances and work with a variety of people. Look at someone like Sir Richard Branson: he's equally adept at mixing it in the boardroom and walking the factory floor. Strong business characters are able to alter their body language, tone and way of speaking so as to mix with all sorts of individuals working in their company. Versatility has been key in getting them to where they today.

THE INTEL

While we're not saying that you should adopt a chameleon-like personality to achieve success in life, there are scenarios when becoming grey can help everybody.

Adapt to your surroundings:

Should you be starting a new job, take note of the atmosphere in the office before you begin. If the company is an internet start-up business, say, and the mood is laidback, arrive in a casual outfit. A more formal establishment should require a suit and tie. It sounds obvious but so many people forget the basics.

Don't rush towards your own death:

In conflicts, such as a heated dispute between colleagues, it sometimes helps to stand back and observe. Don't jump in and say something you might regret later on. Make your points clearly and calmly when the dust settles. Before you decide to intervene, clear your mind and slow the situation down.

Make a grey impression:

Nobody likes a try-hard, especially when they've arrived in a new role or job. Rather than attempting to dazzle your new colleagues with your witty gags and love for an after-work drink, make a conscious effort to blend in subtly and professionally – in those early weeks do your job effectively and engage with others as required rather than acting as the instigator. After all, making a bad impression is far worse than making a grey one.

31

HOW TO ANSWER QUESTIONS UNDER PRESSURE

All of us will have to face questioning to some degree or another during our lives. Those split seconds after a minor car accident can determine how our insurance comes into play. Likewise, an appraisal at work, and how we respond to criticism, might alter our chances of promotion. But answering questions when the pressure is on is a skill we can all master.

FOXY: Getting interrogated isn't nice, believe me, and I've only been questioned under capture during SAS Selection, rather than in a real-life conflict, when the gloves tend to come off. But even in that diluted position when, deep down, I knew that nothing terrible was going to happen, it would have been easy to feel intimidated, forcing me to reveal snippets of information that might compromise me later on. These situations can arise in civilian life, too: moments when we're pressurised into revealing information or making decisions that could have negative implications for us in the future. Examples could include:

- When you might have a secret that affects a lot of people around you.
- When you're the subject of disciplinary action and you don't want to give too much information away.
- In an environment where somebody is pressing you for a company secret.
- The always stressful assigning of blame after a car smash.
- The fallout after a work cock-up.

It's important to always think clearly in these situations, as saying the wrong thing or acting in haste under pressure might cause problems for us – and others – at another time. Let me explain how.

THE VALUE OF DISCRETION AND SECRECY

Knowledge is power, especially in business, where everybody is trying to get the edge on a rival or two, even at the lowest level. Because of the nature of modern industry, with people coming into contact with their peers and adversaries from other companies at meetings, conferences and social functions, it's easy to find ourselves encountering people who might benefit from a single slip. Revealing vital info on our working practices is a real risk, especially when the booze is flying around.

In life, we will always find ourselves privy to private info that could be deemed valuable by another person or party. And we will often be put under pressure to reveal it. In the Special Forces we called the interogation process Tactical Questioning. Often we would pick up an enemy fighter and press him for details on the area or the conflict we had found ourselves in: the position of a key target, where a weapons stash was being held or the likelihood of us encountering IEDs in a nearby field, for example. Often, we did this form of questioning while rounds were zipping around us and everything was going noisy, which would make our captive feel very, very uncomfortable.

Most of the time they were untrained and we could extract intel without too much effort. But I learned to treat each situation as a unique event, and read it accordingly. So when, for instance, someone reacted extremely badly to our aggressiveness and clammed up, I knew it was better to adjust my approach. Rather than shouting in their face I would take a gentler tone; I would empathise, and tell the prisoner that

I understood their predicament and how telling us what we needed to know would help them to get out of there much quicker.

I was always mentally prepared for being captured by the enemy; I knew how I would handle their equivalent of Tactical Questioning. I understood that if I got caught, the people holding me would go to town if they discovered I was a Special Forces soldier: I was a strategic asset. I would probably have been tortured for information and vital secrets. I also knew that if I denied everything and pretended to be a person of low value, then I was highly likely to be killed because I would be deemed useless. The trick, as in a lot of situations where we're being pressed for info when we need to keep secrets, is to give our interrogators enough detail to make them feel as if they have scored some juicy intel when, in reality, it is fairly useless.

Flip that into a civilian situation. You've been entrusted with a secret that affects your entire team, but you've been sworn to secrecy. Or maybe an associate from a rival company starts digging for info after a few drinks. Always have a well-rehearsed story for those moments. Give away enough interesting information to satisfy their curiosity, stuff that you know to be inconsequential or available elsewhere. And keep your secrets closely guarded.

ANSWERING QUESTIONS UNDER PRESSURE

Sometimes Tactical Questioning can take place in extreme conditions. In a war setting, it might be that a Special Forces soldier has been captured and is being tortured for information. In a civilian sense it could be that we've been put on the spot in a highly pressurised situation; a boardroom debrief, say, or during a heated dispute with a colleague. Questions and accusations fly around; people are made the scapegoats for errors, or 'harshed'. One wrong word could lead to recriminations, especially in an argument that might last no more than a minute. Meanwhile, keeping a cool head feels almost impossible. So, what's the answer?

Well, as with all stressful scenarios, we should first slow everything down. Take cover. *Breathe. Recalibrate. Deliver.* Only then can we move forward in a positive fashion, though one surefire way of delivering information in a controlled way is to avoid using the words 'yes' or 'no'. It's quite common for us to be asked a question at a flashpoint which we then answer definitively, only for the conflict to escalate because we've not been able to explain our answer in full. Somebody might ask us, 'Did you sign for that piece of broken equipment?' If we give a definitive answer, without explanation, it can be held against us; a rash decision has been made, which might subsequently have serious implications.

Instead, it's far better to employ phrases such as 'I believe I did' and 'I'm not sure I did', or, in this example, 'I signed for the equipment because it had been checked by a colleague moments earlier and he assured me it was in working order.' That technique was used to great effect by Ollie, recruit no. 3, during Season One of *SAS: Who Dares Wins*. Ollie had made it to the very end of the week and was being put through his paces during the Survive, Evade, Resist, Extract part of the show. He was tired by then, as were all three of the remaining recruits. It would have been easy for him to have mentally collapsed during Tactical Questioning and answered questions with a simple yes or no, but that might have led him into a nasty situation.

Throughout his interrogation, Ollie remained calm. He was polite and managed to sound confident, even though he was involved in a real psychological shit storm.

Interrogator: 'You've not used those mess tins, have you?'

Ollie: 'They're pretty clean.'

Interrogator: 'Do you need those shoes for your feet now?'

Ollie: 'I don't need those for my feet.'

Interrogator: 'Have we missed anything off your inventory list there?'

Ollie: 'I don't think you've missed anything off.'

For soldiers in the Special Forces, there is a far darker motivation for avoiding the use of the words 'yes' or 'no' during an interrogation. Beyond giving away key intel, those interviews are often filmed for propaganda purposes. Usually, yes or no answers are manipulated so that they answer questions that were never asked, such as 'Did you blow up that building full of civilians?' The same is true of signatures. Putting your name to a letter confessing to a war crime that you didn't commit is never a good move, though that's easier said then done when a knife is being held to your throat.

Luckily, that's something you're unlikely to experience.

THE INTEL

During a period of Tactical Questioning:

- Act interested and enthusiastic.
- Have a story prepared in advance, and stick to it.
- Deliver quantity, not quality: a splurge of juicy-sounding but ultimately useless info that will lead your questioner to believe you are someone of interest. It won't make you out to be defensive or a liar.

While under extreme questioning:

- Slow the situation down.
- Remain calm. Talk clearly and with confidence.
- Answer questions with open-ended or ambiguous statements – don't paint yourself into a corner.

32

THE ARMY OF ONE

We all judge ourselves against the achievements of others, good and bad. But the key to maximising our full potential as leaders is not to work to a measuring stick set by someone else. It's to turn our focus inwards and work to our full potential.

COLIN: The Jungle Phase of the Selection process is designed to test the skills of a soldier in two ways. The first is an examination of 'general admin' – how somebody cares for their equipment and themselves. If one team member doesn't clean their weapon properly, they will inevitably end up failing. Ignoring personal hygiene in extreme conditions will cause someone's health to deteriorate, and fast. Somebody might catch a horrible disease: a skin infection in the foot can result in rot and, in the worst case, amputation. Soldiers will get found out pretty quickly if they don't look after themseves in the jungle.

The second element of the Jungle Phase is good soldiering, which includes general field craft, camouflage, tactics and contact drills, in which we engage with teams posing as enemy groups. A recruit who's not slick with their weapon or is unable to move quickly and aggressively will soon flash up on the DS's radar as being unsuitable. Meanwhile, standard skills are constantly placed under the microscope. For example, you don't have to be a rocket scientist to pass the map-reading course in the Hills Phase. You only have to look to the highest peak to see a trail of soldiers wearing bergens, all of them running to the top. But jungle maps are recorded from a plane, which flies over the trees and sometimes the cartographers rely on guesswork. Landmarks are judged on the height of the canopy and often the map doesn't match the terrain underneath. So guess what? You're in trouble before you've even started, which can create a tricky test of confidence and ability.

My work on the Jungle Phase began before we made our first moves through the vegetation, the heat and the wet. In the Special Forces we use a lot of mnemonics and one of these is 'Shape, Shine, Shadow, Silhouette and Movement', so if you're the wrong shape while hiding in the bushes that might give your position away. Likewise, if you've got shine on your person, such as a piece of equipment that glints in the sunlight, or if you're creating shadows or silhouettes, or making any movement, noise or smell. All of these would be considered examples of poor admin and they had to be prepared for. Before I went in, I didn't wash, or brush my teeth, for a week because I knew that a tracker – a member of the DS installed to trail us and watch our every move – could smell toothpaste and soap from 100 metres away.

In these conditions, the soldiers worked on top of one another, waking just before dawn. We would get out of our dry kit, and into the wet gear, putting on camouflage cream and fixing our weapons before the sun had crept above the horizon (not that we could see it that well). Our equipment had to be primed and ready to go before our unit could set out, and that's when the work got seriously tough: during the day we would sweat our way up and down the gradients, hacking through primary jungle, executing attacks, and performing reccies and observations. It was exhausting.

Every single soldier on the Jungle Phase was being assessed 24/7, even when he was asleep. It was stressful, especially for me, because it was my first time in that environment – I had been thrown in at the deep end. But not everybody was like me. Some of the other candidates had been through Selection before. Others had previously trained in the jungle, and one or two of my colleagues were even jungle warfare instructors. There were also people in my unit who were stronger than me, fitter than me, more intelligent than me. But I was the one who made it to the end – they didn't.

My route to success? I made the decision to maintain

my inner focus. I concentrated on what *I* was doing rather than watching the achievements and performances of the people around me. I guessed that if I stopped to survey my colleagues – the tough, the injured, the effective and the moaners – I wouldn't make it through, especially if I judged myself by their standards. If I watched the weaker people going through hell, it might trick my mind into contemplating an early exit. Studying a stronger person might have crumpled my self-belief because I wasn't matching their performance. Instead, I concentrated on my own work and functioned to the best of my ability. I knew I was already there on merit. If I worked to my capabilities, I would finish the phase.

I focused on the hour-to-hour, the day-to-day. I did what I could to get through those timescales effectively and successfully. Before I knew it, I was through the jungle and ticking the box. I'd made it through another stage.

THE INTEL

This mindset doesn't just apply to military personnel: it can be effectively utilised by somebody starting a new job or an individual who wants to lose weight as part of a group effort; you might even be a student in the middle of exams. In these situations it's easy to get caught up in how your friends or peers are doing. Certain people will talk about how they're nailing it, hitting their targets every week and cruising through. But focusing on the people ahead of you in the game will stress you out. Meanwhile, paying too much attention to the poor performers being left behind could be just as damaging, if you compare yourself to them and start thinking, 'Hang on, this is really tough.' Or, worse, you risk becoming complacent. When you think you're doing better than everybody else there is a chance you won't achieve your full potential. Fear can be debilitating, while reassurance might lull you into a false sense of security.

Likewise, if you're a parent, you can become caught in a vicious trap when eternally comparing your own kid to your friends' children. Are they as successful? Are they as smart? Are they as happy? Then, inevitably, you start to ask, 'Compared to the people I see at the school gates every day, am I a good parent?' But judging personal standards by the performances of others is poor practice. It creates a sense of inferiority at one end of the spectrum and complacency at the other. It can draw you away from your own priorities and goals, rob you of any sense of perspective, and leave you grappling with things over which you have no influence. Instead, focus on yourself: be your own benchmark.

Become your Army of One.

33
THE VALUE OF GOOD ADMIN

Admin: it's a word we use all the time in the military and it can be applied to a variety of situations. How you care for your kit can be categorised as 'admin'. Likewise, personal hygiene, preparing Target Packs or planning missions. It's all classed as administration, and how you manage it can sometimes be the difference between life and death. But civilian leaders should understand the important of good admin, too. It can save us time and improve our efficiency, whatever the situation.

COLIN: One of the oldest Army mottos in the book is 'My weapon, my kit, myself'. That means you take care of your weapon first, then your equipment and finally your personal requirements, such as food and water or personal hygiene. It's no good just being fed, watered and rot-free; it's no good just having a shiny set of kit. If our weapons don't work and we encounter the enemy, all of us are dead. The Army prioritises weapons for a reason.

During the Jungle Phase of Selection, everything was damp and covered in crap from the vegetation and humidity, which meant that keeping our guns in pristine condition would be extra hard. Every morning we would wake in the dark, crawling from our hammocks and packing down our camp. Then I would lie down, flat on my back, my bergen resting underneath me as I cleaned my gun. Even when we were working our way through the primary jungle, I would always clean my gun whenever I had the chance, just to make sure. I knew that if I didn't, there was a chance it might fail me when I needed it most. That was good admin.

A little bit of extra admin on my kit could also save me a hell of a lot of time, especially when managing so much equipment in tricky circumstances. To keep ourselves from contracting debilitating water-borne diseases, we would use purifying tablets, or 'puritabs', to clean our drinking water, which was often scooped up in water bottles from nearby rivers. The tablets were a pain in the arse, though. They arrived in card packets, like your typical pill dispensers and we had to rip them open, while still holding our rifles* and navigating the terrain.

I had watched soldiers struggling with them in the past, attempting to rip open the packets as they moved forward, sometimes breaking the puritab, other times getting it right, but I realised it was costing them valuable time, while taking their focus off the job in hand, albeit briefly. Before moving into the jungle, I sat down with my kit and opened up the whole packet, dropping all 200 puritabs into a small tub. I then stuffed the tub with cotton wool, so the pills wouldn't make a rattling noise, and covered the whole tub in green sniper paint as camouflage.

These small details were vital because of the trackers who were following us to assess us. Believe me, those guys were the best in the business. They could pick up our trail from the smallest clues, such as a broken leaf. We were walking along trails unaware that anyone had been watching us, but

---

*   ANT: We were trained not to take a hand off our weapon when advancing through tricky conditions. I remember our patrol crossing a river during the Jungle Phase. To get over, we had to navigate a fallen log, and the way the branches had landed created what looked like a handrail. (It later turned out to be a trap. The DS had deliberately cut the wood that way.) When I saw it, I thought, 'There's going to be someone in these trees . . .'

Suddenly, the bloke in front of my put his hand out for balance, grabbing the rail. Within seconds, there was a shout from the woods. It was one of the DS who had been tracking us.

'Oi! *You!*' he shouted. 'Both hands on the weapon!'

When I looked across, he was scribbling in his notepad, marking down the soldier's name.

when we got back to base at the end of the phase, they had been on our tail all along. Their reports were full of intel on where we had been, how many of us were in the squadron; they would even list what side each shoulder carried their weapon. To those trackers, a rattling pillbox would have been like an air raid siren going off.

Finally, there's the admin of personal health. As you can imagine, there are all sorts of infections to bring a person down during the Jungle Phase. We're in and out of the water all day long, and because of the humid conditions it's almost impossible for us to dry out. If soldiers don't take good care of their feet, for example, they'll contract trench foot and fungal rot. Now, that's manageable at first, if a little uncomfortable. But after two weeks the skin starts to split open. Bleeding sores get infected after a while and it becomes impossible to walk.

Casualties are a big deal in the jungle because of the effort required to rescue them. If someone breaks a leg during an Immediate Action drill, an ambulance isn't going to come along to drive the injured soldier to a nearby hospital. The Special Forces Jungle Phase takes place hundreds of miles away from civilisation, so the squadron has to literally drag an injured recruit through the vegetation until they're able to create a winch hole. This is done by cutting down a tree and making a small gap in the forest canopy, so a helicopter can send a rope down to whisk the soldier away.

That's why the small details are so vital. The Jungle Phase is an equaliser. I'm not going to say that it separates the dross from the elite, because some great soldiers turn up for that part of the Selection process and fail. Instead, it exposes the people that aren't fit enough, robust enough or practical enough to make the grade. In conditions as tough as those, soldiers with a strong understanding of personal admin can find an edge.

THE INTEL

Knowing how to best improve our levels of admin is a personal action – no one else can do it for us. Only we can understand how best to upgrade our living and working conditions, because we're the ones losing time and focus due to poor practice. How to narrow this down is best done through the military motto I mentioned earlier: 'My weapon, my kit, myself'. Apply each category to your own situation.

My weapon

For any Special Forces operative, the gun is our most valuable piece of equipment. Without it, our risk of survival in a conflict diminishes greatly. In the civilian world, each of us has an equivalent – it's the asset that best shapes our trade or job. For many of us, it's a computer or laptop, but it could also be a taxi driver's car, a photographer's camera or a salesperson's contacts file.

Identify your most valuable working asset or assets, and prioritise their maintenance. After all, if a soldier's gun isn't cared for and jams during a firefight, it's unlikely their day is going to end well. Take it as read that if you don't care for your most important piece of equipment, it might fail you when you need it most.

My kit

We all understand the weaknesses in our working processes, the places where we can best save time and work more effectively. It could be that our desk is a mess and important resources are difficult to locate in vital moments. Maybe our inbox is overflowing with junk email, making it harder to spot the important stuff coming through; the space where we store our tools might be in disarray. Overall, though, like my prepared puritabs in the jungle, there are always various measures that can be taken to speed up the mechanics of your job. Tidy the tool cupboard, delete the irrelevant emails and save yourself a potential headache.

Myself

Take this as a general category regarding the organisation of your day-to-day activities, rather than any preventative measures for foot rot or tropical diseases. If you want a visual representation of what I'm talking about here, consider the movie *The Airport*. There's a scene in it in which several businessmen cruise through security. They have their passports at the ready. Their bags have been packed effectively. Their kit's in order and they know where everything is. As a result, they're able to glide from checkpoint to checkpoint without any problem or delay.

Next up we see an American family. They've forgotten to pack several important documents. They want to stop for coffee, even though time is perilously short. Inevitably, they end up racing through security in a blind panic. The Special Forces attitude to admin, and personal organisation, is like the businessmen in that movie. Everything is prepared in advance so we can work effectively and slickly.

DEBRIEF

Make no mistake about it: passing into the Special Forces is arguably the greatest achievement any soldier can make in their career. Once that status has been attained there's an honour in knowing that you're one of the best, working alongside the most adept technicians in the business. But in reality the job has only just begun. Only once we've put the techniques developed within Selection, training and 'Add Quals' can we fulfil our potential. The really hard work is yet to come.

The same applies to you and your approach to *SAS: Who Dares Wins – Leadership Secrets from the Special Forces.* During these pages, we've given you the techniques and tools to operate to the best of your ability; to become elite in whatever walk of life you work in. You now have a functional path to mission delivery in play; operating to the best of your ability when life gets noisy is within reach; understanding teamwork and management issues will become easier; you can now operate like a Thinking Soldier.

How you use this armoury is up to you. The book has been designed to serve as an easily digestible manual, which you can refer back to whenever necessary. Meanwhile, the intel section of each chapter is your shorthand guide for times when quick and decisive action is key. Overall, though, you possess a framework in which to improve your leadership skills. In military terms, you have completed the training phase.

It's time to step into action for real: you're in the thick of it now.

Breathe.

Recalibrate.

Deliver.

THE DS